The First Element

Secrets to Maximizing Your Energy

The First Element

Secrets to Maximizing Your Energy

by
Grandmaster
Tae Yun Kim

NORTHSTAR

Copyright © 1999 by Grandmaster Tae Yun Kim
Published by NorthStar
119 Minnis Circle
Milpitas, CA 95035
(408) 942-3307
www.gonorthstar.com

Cover design: Keoki Williams
Text design & typography: *Easy Break*™

1. Self-help/management, 2. Personal relationships,
3. Stress reduction/management, 4. Philosophy,
5. Wholistic Health, 6. Energy Management,
7. Martial Arts

ISBN: 0-9656959-0-5
LCCN: 97-66383

First printing, January, 1999

Printed in the USA on recycled acid-free paper

NOTE

The power of Ki energy can be a tremendous force in your life, but it is not to be confused as any sort of religion or religious belief. Ki can be incorporated into your life in tandem with any religious beliefs you may or may not hold. Through development of your mind, body, and spirit, you can connect with your inner voice and will be able to increase your connection to any universal or religious philosophies that you follow.

The techniques, ideas and suggestions in this book are not intended as a substitute for proper medical advice. Any application of the techniques, ideas, and suggestions in this book is at the reader's sole discretion and risk.

Acknowledgments

I thank God from the bottom of my heart for sending me to this world and allowing me to become a student as well as a teacher. Through my personal experiences I have learned to rejoice in the lessons of life. They have made me stronger and given me the freedom to become who I am today.

I give thanks to my great teacher and Master in life, Jesus Christ, who helps me celebrate each living breath as if it were my last. I give special thanks to my team: Scott H. Salton, Michael B. Fell, Thomas Saunders, Mark Amador, Adam Giandomenico, Erika Sommers, Kristina Williams, and Sarah Kim.

I am blessed by all the people I have come into contact with, and will come in contact with, for they have and will help mold me into the person I am today. I thank you all.

God bless you,

Grandmaster Tae Yun Kim

Grandmaster Tae Yun Kim,
founder of the art of Jung SuWon,
dressed in a traditional long, flowing robe,
moves gracefully, fluidly, powerfully, gently, sometimes swiftly,
but also calmly,
through a series of energetic Ki rhythm movements
called a form.
A rapt audience of several thousand now watches her close her eyes
and enter a motionless and serenely quiet meditative state.
Two students set a bed of nails behind her,
and one of them tosses an apple onto the nails.
The apple is pierced through!
A murmur of excitement spreads through the audience
as their anxious anticipation heightens.
Grandmaster is unmoved.
Smiling, she opens her eyes.
She is resolute, still, focused, detached.
The students lift her rigid body onto the bed of nails,
and six cinder blocks are placed on her stomach,
one on top of the other.
A student approaches and stands over her
with a large sledge hammer.
He raises the hammer. He's counting. The hammer is coming down!
The shout of his ki-up pierces the silence
as he strikes the cinder blocks,
now exploding in a shower of stones,
settling in a rubble all around her.
The breathless audience gasps in response...
Will she get up? Is she hurt?
How can she withstand the energy of that blow
without being pierced like the apple?
But she is lifted out of the rubble, and far from being hurt,
she again goes through the artful motions of a form,
arms and legs gracefully whirling from one stance to another,
smiling, unharmed, unmarked, alert, aware, as energetic as before.
Now the form comes to a close.
Charged with tingling emotions of relief, admiration,
and appreciation,
the audience spontaneously jumps to their feet,
enthusiastically applauding her demonstration in a standing ovation.
Grandmaster puts her hands together softly and returns their respect
with a gentle bow.
Oakland Coliseum, 1991

Table of Contents

The First Element

Introduction

Energy. How many times a day do you hear that word? Offices, restaurants, schools, everywhere you find people together, you hear people talking about energy:

That was a wonderful aerobics class, great energy!
The energy in this music is so exciting.
I love to be around Susan's energy when I'm depressed.
Did you feel the hostile energy in the meeting yesterday?
Those colors are too low energy for this room...
What can we do to energize this project and get it going?
Mr. Lee's lectures are so high energy you don't get tired.

When I do a demonstration such as described previously, I am actually working with different forms of energy, which we will discuss in greater detail throughout this book.

Yes, energy takes more than one form in this world we live in. Although you may never have consciously defined energy, you certainly feel it come and go and affect you in many different ways. That is why you can talk about it so easily even though you don't really know what it is.

But what is it?

Where does it come from? How is it we use this word to describe everything from nuclear power, to colors, to emotions? And most importantly for readers of this book, what does energy mean in terms of understanding your own personal body, mind, spirit? What does energy mean in terms of interacting with your environment, forming relationships, and creating your life? When you finish this book, my hope is that you will know much more about the nature of your own energy, and how to use it to create a life fulfilling your deepest desires.

There is a universal Creative Force which brought the universe into existence. It also brought you into being. What is the essence of this Creative Force? What is it made of? Energy.

The First Element

The universal Creative Force is energy, which takes form as your individuality, your body, your mind, your spirit, your life, and your world. This energy is called *ki* in many eastern traditions (pronounced key, and sometimes spelled *qi*), *prana* in Indian or Hindu traditions, *chi* by the Chinese, and more recently *life force* in the west.

You and this creative life force of the universe - you and this original ki - are unified, fused together as the same field of energy. *Silent Master* or *Silent Master Consciousness* is the expression I use to describe this original, pure life force as it exists within you personally. So your Silent Master is your original Self, made of original universal creative energy; and you *are* this Self right now. Your physical Self is just one part of your total energy field. But if you aren't aware that you are this universal ki energy...if you don't know how much power is in this energy...if you don't know you can direct this energy...if you don't know, in short, that your Silent Master is your true, original Self, and the source of your personal ki energy...then you are most likely limiting your creative abilities. On the other hand, if you are consciously aware of how to tap into your Silent Master Consciousness - and *direct* your pure ki energy - you might achieve far more than you presently dream possible.

In doing the bed of nails demonstration, I like to show people how limited their concept of energy might be. During that time, there are a lot of different energies coming at me all at once. Gravity is pushing my back against the nails; biological energy is beating my heart and keeping my vital functions going; the potential energy of the material sledge hammer poised in the air is rapidly changing into powerful kinetic energy as it slams into the cinder blocks on my stomach; my mental energy is aware of this entire proceeding and of the necessity to protect myself; and my emotional energy is feeling possible dangerous consequences.

If I were to focus *only* on these energies, I could be limited to many commonly accepted expectations surrounding these energies. Let's say one general expectation is that gravity, plus my body weight, plus the force of the sledge hammer *should* cause the nails to puncture my back or at least hurt me. The general expectation surrounding my mental energy is that I *should* know better than to put myself in that dangerous situation and I *should* get out of it, and the expectation surrounding my emotional energy is that I *should* be afraid. So many "shoulds"! I break what many people consider "rules," and yet I do not suffer any consequences. Why do you think this is?

The reason is, in my meditative state, I rise to my Silent Master Consciousness, where I am aware that my original ki is more powerful than these more limited forms of energy. These limited forms of energy are subject to my control when I focus myself in my "higher" Silent Master energy, and I cannot get hurt.

Although this bed of nails demonstration shows that we can exercise more control over energies than we might have thought possible, there are far more important issues in your life. For instance, what accepted expectations are pinning down your life right now? Do the "rules" say that because you lost your job, there's no way to make a living now? Do you have a general expectation that you can't have a successful relationship? Or a fulfilling career? Or a healthier, more attractive body? Do you think you have some good "reasons" why you should be more limited than you desire to be? If so, it may be time to stand up to the sledge hammer coming down in your life, and demonstrate that you can utilize your own Silent Master energy to overcome limitation in your life! It may be time to awaken your original ki, and learn how to purify and direct it.

Everything created was born out of the original universal life force and exists now as some form of energy. So in order to exercise your ability to create the life you want, you need to exercise your energy! Your ki is literally the key to shaping your life into the naturally fulfilling adventure you want it to be.

In the following chapters, my goal is to help you achieve a better understanding of your own ki so you can begin consciously developing and directing it. We will approach ki from six different directions, each of which points to some area where ki is the key to creating freedom, happiness, and health.

Ki is the key to:

1. *energizing yourself* with the pure, original creative life force of the universe, so you feel bright, vibrant, expressive and powerful.
2. *transforming yourself*, creating the mind, body, and life you've always wanted.
3. *radiating positive energy into your environment*, so that you reduce stress and discord, and promote peace and harmony.
4. *forming great relationships* where you enjoy love without dependency and express individuality without conflict.
5. *staying healthy*, feeling young, strong, and well balanced physically, emotionally, mentally, spiritually.
6. *taking charge* of your life so that you are a creator and an actor on your life path rather than a victim and a reactor.

Hopefully, as we go through these six different areas, you will emerge with a much deeper and expanded concept of energy! There's no doubt that energy is a popular buzzword in today's world. All you have to do is watch a few minutes of commercial advertising on television and you can see the value we place on "high energy." Cars, blue jeans, orange juice, batteries, soft drinks, even laundry detergents, you name it, are portrayed with dazzling images of highly energized joy and vitality. Yet, is this your actual experience of energy in the environment of your everyday world? Probably not. The source of this kind of joy and energy is deeper than these television images portray. And certainly those images won't automatically bring you instantaneous bubbling happiness and energy, although that is what the advertiser wants you to believe!

No, if you really want spontaneous joy, true happiness, and high energy, you must go to its true source: the pure original ki of your Silent Master Consciousness. And this will undoubtedly require effort, persistence, and training on your part. The martial art I created, Jung SuWon, means "the way of uniting body, mind, and spirit in total harmony." Since Jung SuWon emphasizes harmony, it emphasizes energy training, because harmony is an energetic state of your Silent Master Consciousness! So is love...so is beauty...so are joy, power, health, and vitality.

The teachings in this book are some of the basics of my Jung SuWon training. Much of this training I give to my students and those who attend my seminars, workshops, and Self-Discovery Weekends. Jung SuWon embraces truths which are also found in many other traditions all over the world. One of my teachers, for instance, was a Buddhist master, but he never hesitated to voice many truths as they appear in the Bible. I, too, occasionally quote Bible passages, not for religious purposes, but because they express universal truths in a beautiful way.

It is my sincere hope that my training and life experiences will help you take a step forward in unlocking your true energy. Your own ki is the key to fulfilling your dreams and discovering your original Self, your Silent Master!

You are energy. Energy is all around you, in you, traveling to you and from you. Energy is all there is! Remember the parable in the Bible about the man who sells all he has to buy the one "pearl of great price"? Your true energy is this pearl. If you commit yourself to finding your Silent Master energy, you will have found the Source of all. What could be more valuable than this?

Even if it's hard work, you can enjoy your walk on this path! I believe that learning who you really are can ultimately be one of life's most pleasurable and most important pursuits.

When your effort and persistence reward you with the peaceful inner joy of expressing your true talents and desires, I believe you'll agree with me. More and more, love who you are and celebrate the beating of your heart as life's gift of energy to you. Value each moment of your life as if it were the last, filling each minute with all the joy you can. My love supports you in every step you take, and my desire is that you discover your pure original being, your Silent Master Consciousness.

Grandmaster Tae Yun Kim

CHAPTER ONE

What Is Ki?

Everywhere I look,
I am already there.
Everywhere I move,
I am already dancing.
Everywhere I feel,
I am already vibrating.
Everywhere I show myself,
I am already Loving.

Ki Is Inner Power

What is ki? In two words, ki is *inner power*! The breath of life, the power of the universal life force manifesting in you.

Later in this chapter I will share with you a story of how one of my students worked to develop his ki power and turned a suicidal life into one filled with joy, radiance, and achievement. Like my student, you can learn to access and increase your ki power. But sometimes it shows its power to you before you even know what it is. Have you heard stories about people who perform amazing feats of strength or endurance, such as a mother who lifts a car off her child trapped underneath? Or perhaps you've heard of a person who walks several miles on a broken leg to seek help...or a feeble person who suddenly finds the strength to break down a door in a fire...or a person with terminal cancer who suddenly experiences total remission.

Perhaps you have had a similar experience, where you unconsciously shifted gears and utilized a powerful energy way beyond your ordinary expectations. You may have marveled afterwards, "Wow, how did I do that?" And maybe you were disappointed to find you couldn't do it again so easily. Maybe you decided your performance was just a fluke.

These instances are usually called "miracles" of one sort or another. But they are actually evidence of an inner power we all possess! Ki power. Ki (pronounced *key*) is an oriental term for energy. Ki in its pure original form is the very life force of the universe, the energy which creates life and sets everything in motion: the swirling of galaxies, the birth of stars, the hatching of an eagle's egg, the blooming of a flower, the infant growing into an adult...All these things are evidence of universal ki energy manifesting as life and motion.

Ki Is Creative

First: it is *creative* energy. Where does our universe come from? Where do you come from? What creates everything? Ki. Ki is all there is, and it transforms itself into you and the universe. That is, ki creatively takes form as - or you could say gives birth to - not only the material universe, but also other kinds of energies which we experience generally as our physical body, our emotions, our mind, and our spirit. You and all the elements of the universe, are born out of this original, universal energy.

Even the so-called man-made objects we construct, such as autos, furniture, and clothing, are made of energy, because they are synthesized from elements appearing naturally in the universe. Nothing, then, is truly man-made. The original universal ki transforms into earth elements, and we transform the earth elements into objects. When man-made objects disintegrate, as all objects do in time, they lose their form and dissolve back into their original energetic elements.

Think about this book you're holding. The ink came from natural earth and minerals. The paper came from a tree, and the tree also came from earth, with the natural sun, water, and air nourishing it. To make this book, we did not create the elements, but simply rearranged them.

Original Ki Is Your Silent Master

The second important thing to know about ki is that this pure, original ki which created the universe is within you right now. You are one with this energy. I call your awareness of this energy presence within you the *Silent Master* or *Silent Master Consciousness*. In my first book, <u>Seven Steps to Inner Power</u>, I described your Silent Master in six "Images." Here are the first three images, which summarize the nature of your connection to the universal life force.

I
YOU ARE ONE OF A KIND

*Your Silent Master is your Real Self,
your original Self. It expresses Itself
through your thinking, through true
Ideas and Thoughts in your mind. It is
your eternal Selfhood that exists apart
from your brain (which is a sensory
processor only) and the personality traits
imposed on you from your environment.*

II
YOU AND THE LIFE FORCE ARE ONE

*Your Silent Master Consciousness was
born out of the infinite Life Force
creating and animating the Universe.
You exist as a part of the Universe;
therefore, It is the Life Force creating
and animating you. It is the power that
beats your heart. Because you are this
Consciousness, whatever qualities the
Life Force possesses, you possess also.*

III
YOUR THOUGHTS CREATE REALITY

*Your Silent Master Consciousness knows
Itself to be immaterial in substance, but
It also takes form (manifests) as your
physical body and the material world
around you. Thus, you may describe
yourself as being both immaterial
(spiritual) and material (physical) at the
same time.*

These three images give you important information about your Silent Master to bear in mind as we continue to discuss ki energy throughout this book. These images tell you how to contact your Silent Master. Where is it? In your own consciousness - not somewhere "out there." Since your Silent Master energy is *aware* within your own mind, you can direct this energy with your mind.

Also, since you and your Silent Master are one, you have the same qualities it has. For instance, since your Silent Master energy is creative, you are creative. You can create a life and environment in accord with your dreams and goals...With your Silent Master's harmony, you can manifest forms of beauty...With your Silent Master's joy, you can experience unconditional happiness...With your Silent Master's love, you can appreciate your unique qualities and your one-of-a-kind individuality...With your Silent Master's power, you can be an actor instead of a reactor or victim.

And you can enjoy and express your Silent Master Consciousness while you are physical. You don't have to give up your physical being to know yourself as a spiritual being. Since everything that exists is a manifestation of original ki energy, you can interact with the energy of your environment and the world around you to forge your own destiny.

You Create Your Life With Ki

So here you are. You are one with the life force of the universe! You possess the same original energy which created the universe! You also possess other types of energies which are born out of your original ki (we talk about those energies in the next chapter), but the most creative and powerful energy you possess is the ki of your Silent Master Consciousness. With your Silent Master energy, you become a co-creator of the world you presently live in, directing your energy to manifest your deepest and truest desires.

Bear in mind that you also use your energy to create the life you don't want! Everything is a manifestation of some form of energy, positive or negative, including situations of poverty, disease, and broken relationships. This is why it's so important to learn about your energy and learn how to use it positively.

In fact, you may wonder how it is that our world is so troublesome - so filled with strife and conflict and unhappiness - when there's this perfect, pure energy available. Why are we not more aware of our Real Self and more aware of the inner power we possess to control the energies around us? Let's find out. Let's use our time together to wake up and start looking for victory in life, not defeat!

Your Ki Can Be Clouded

The time when our original self is the most clear and strong is when we are small children. If you watch small children at play - their joyful abandon, their spontaneous imagination, their unbounded energy and self-acceptance, their natural trust and their willingness to accept love and to love unconditionally - it's not surprising that Jesus said, "unless you become as a little child, you cannot enter the kingdom of God." But this is also the time when we are most vulnerable, helplessly dependent on adults who may have been hurt and damaged themselves as children. In some cases, sometimes knowingly, sometimes unknowingly, sometimes in big ways, sometimes in small ways, these damaged people can pass their fear and pain on to their children.

Some of us may feel that when we were children we received damaging messages that said: "I can't be who I am without arousing fear, competition, jealousy, or resentment...I have to fulfill *others'* expectations for me in order to survive...I can't express my feelings without fear of retaliation...I can't trust other people...My needs aren't as important as everyone else's needs...Being 'different' creates rejection or conflict...."

I am not condemning parenthood or families in any way. Many families are a powerful source of love and support. But some of us were born into families where one or both of the parents had unresolved pain and conflict from their own childhood, and this situation can create a vicious cycle that can be passed on from parent to child - mostly unintentionally - until we make an effort to consciously wake up and heal ourselves in order to create our own freedom and individuality!

Is it time for you to do this?

You Can Change Your Life With Ki

One of my students, whom I'll call Robert, is a good example of someone who believed he had to accept a lot of pain and limitation because "that's just the way life is." He had reached the point of not wanting to live. As far as he could see, why stay alive in a world so hurtful?

Robert was raised in a family where communication, such as ordinary dinner conversations or sharing feelings or expressing opinions or showing affection, was unvalued and not allowed. The belief was that children are "accidents" that happen. Children definitely have nothing important to say, and should stay out of the way without needing, wanting, or asking for anything. He learned at an early age that if he expressed his true thoughts or opinions, especially if they disagreed with those of his parents, he would encounter condemnation, anger, or some kind of hostile retaliation. If he ever ventured to confide some personal information in his parents, the information would later be used against him to deride or humiliate him. He learned that when he showed strong emotion, the power of his feelings aroused fear in his parents, and they would take punitive action to stamp out - rather than redirect - his anger, sadness, or pain. And when he was old enough to begin feeling his sexuality, his parents did nothing to support this change happening in his life, did nothing to encourage healthy interaction with girls his age,

7

and coldly avoided the subject of sex or any issues related to sexuality.

Put yourself in Robert's place. What were the only logical conclusions he could come to about himself? "It's wrong to talk, so I shouldn't...It's dangerous to feel, so I can't...It's futile to express myself, so I won't...It's wrong to touch, so I'll withdraw...My body is insignificant, so I'll degenerate...There's no one I can relate to...So I'm alone...I'm cold...I'm empty...I'm a shell...with nothing to create, nothing to contribute, nothing to anticipate..."

Can you imagine what it would be like to live in such a hollow space? I don't think Robert's parents treated him in a way they thought was damaging. Since they saw no reason to question their values or change their behavior, they probably believed they were "normal" parents. Very likely they treated Robert the way their parents treated them.

As I mentioned previously, everything in your life is energy: your thoughts, emotions, sexuality, physicality, everything. When these energies are suppressed, as they were in Robert's situation, they don't just "go away." Instead, they find their own outlet, one which may not be to your liking. It was no surprise to me to learn that Robert had also developed epilepsy. To put it simply, I believe that epilepsy could be a physical expression of neurological energy that goes "out of control" and erupts wildly into involuntary "seizures." There could be a connection between his emotional suppression and the epilepsy he developed - that epilepsy could be a picture of how unexpressed energy builds up and then simply explodes on its own. I knew that ki could greatly enhance the traditional medical treatment he was receiving.

So in addition to being alone and empty, Robert had epilepsy to contend with. By the time he entered college, he had already set himself in a pattern of social withdrawal. He lived by himself, never talked to anyone, had few friends, and found his only company in books, which he read by the hundreds. The only world that was safe for him was a fantasy world, an escape he found in the black and white pages of novels. As another way of escaping, he slept ten to fifteen hours a night.

Then episodes of severe depression began. Again, there's only so long one can seek a numb "escape" from the energies of life. This time for Robert, the unexpressed energies collected into powerful feelings of depression, which then accelerated into a negative outlet: thoughts of suicide.

Just as he was at the point of seriously contemplating this action, he happened to tag along with some friends to one of my Self-Discovery Weekends. These weekends are two full days of energy exercises designed to help people break through physical, emotional, and mental blocks. Robert remained completely withdrawn throughout the weekend, watching the events as though imprisoned behind glass walls. It wasn't until the last few minutes of the last exercise that he began to respond. Emotions of great sadness finally shook through his weak and frail body in a torrent of tears and sobbing. I was thrilled because this was probably one of the first real, constructive expressions of energy that he'd had in years!

This marked the beginning of his Jung SuWon training with me. I knew that our work together would be a process of encouraging him to express more and more aspects of his entire energy field, physically, emotionally, mentally, and spiritually. Occasionally in this work, he would have an epileptic seizure that appeared to be connected to a block of suppressed energy that we had hit upon during class. Since he hadn't learned to handle the energy released from the block, it appeared as if the energy was being expressed through the seizure. I knew that I could help him to gain the confidence to confront and control the negative energy, rather than let it control him, and that this would be a great support to his traditional medical treatment.

The physical martial arts training was having a good effect on his physical, emotional, and mental energy, but I also extended his ki energy program with special recommendations for diet, meditation exercises, and ki rhythm movements. As he worked in these areas, he began to see substantial growth and transformation. Slowly over time, the seizures began to diminish. He became more aware of his emotions and let them be expressed openly and constructively. Other students watching his transformation were excited and inspired by his progress.

Before too long, he developed a desire to expand his career interests. He loved gadgets and constructing electrical components but had never trained in electrical engineering, something which he'd always wanted to do. I wasn't surprised at his new desire for a better career, because for the first time, Robert's energy was being *released* and *expressed* instead of being suffocated. When energy is freed up, you naturally want to do something with it! And it was quite natural that he started creating a different life with his new energy - rather than escaping and slowly dying as before. He changed his studies at college to be more in line with his new goals.

He continues to train and is developing a body that is vibrant, strong, expressive, and healthy, free of epileptic seizures. One of the signs of his enhanced energy is that he now sleeps only around five hours a night.

What a turnaround! But this story is only one of many instances I have encountered where energy training completely reclaimed someone's life. As I said, everything is energy; and if you want to change your circumstances, you must alter the energy in your being and environment.

Ki Belongs to Everyone

Western medicine is slowly becoming aware of the energetic nature of healing. In the East, however, disease has been recognized as unbalanced energy for centuries, and eastern healing methods, such as acupressure and acupuncture, have been used to rebalance disrupted energy patterns in the body so that healing results. So the science and study of ki energy is nothing new! Western medicine and psychology, generally speaking, simply don't incorporate an awareness of how ki energy supplements life systems.

However, this has been changing recently. Some of the "discoveries" being made in the area of energy - such as how visualization exercises can help cancer patients boost their immune systems - are actually "uncoveries." That is, the power of energy exercises have always been there; the modern world is not inventing these ideas, but rather uncovering their existence.

When I first came to this country and spoke of meditation, I heard people say, "Don't meditate: you will lose your mind." I couldn't even attempt to speak about energy or meditation except with senior students who had trained long enough to trust and actually experience what I was talking about. Now I find a growing audience receptive to the idea of meditation. More and more people today are awakening and opening their mind to the power within them and, in fact, are hungry for ways to understand and explore themselves.

In the rest of this book, we will be looking specifically at how your ki impacts your body, relationships, environment, and health, and how to direct your ki in taking charge of your life. I'd like you to feel able to alter your energy in positive ways by the time you finish this book...and not unlike my student, Robert, experience the beginning of a new start in finding out who you really are and what you can really accomplish.

But first, in this chapter, I would like to give you a little more background on the concept of ki. The fuller your understanding of ki, the fuller your experience of it will be.

In a few words, here are the three concepts I'll be talking about in the rest of this chapter:
1. Ki vibrates.
2. Different frequencies of vibration produce different energies.
3. Ki can transform itself into different energies - environmental, physical, emotional, mental, and

spiritual - because it can change its speed of vibration (its frequency).

If these three concepts come easily to you, you can skip on to Chapter Two, where we get right down to using energy to shape and develop your individual self. You don't need the information in the rest of this chapter to learn how to take charge of your energy and create a brand new life! If you're curious as to *why* ki vibrates and *how* it transforms into different energies you possess, I encourage you to reach for a deeper concept and understanding of ki.

The vibrating nature of ki is the key to understanding why it's *energetic*. Isn't it interesting that the English language reflects the vibrating nature of our energy? When we talk about energy around us, we refer to feeling "vibes." When we are with other people in a particular environment, we may talk about having "good vibes" or "bad vibes," "peaceful vibes" or "hostile vibes." We may refer to someone as being "vibrant" or "radiant," which is also a comment on the vibrational quality of their energy.

If you're interested in why this is so, get out your magnifying glass and let's look deeper into why energy works this way.

Why Is Ki Energetic?

To answer this question, we might first ask another question: Where does energy come from? If we know where something comes from - if we know something about its source - that sometimes tells us something about it. Does ki have the characteristics of its source? Yes, absolutely! So what is the source of ki like?

The source of ki is what the Chinese call the Tao. The Tao is the Source of all, the "parent" of everything that exists potentially and everything that exists actually. What does Tao mean? It means a "Way." So if the Source of ki is a "way," we must now look more closely at that word, *way*...

What is a way? A way is by nature a process, something in motion, changing from one state to another. When you follow the way to the supermarket, you are *constantly changing* your position to get there. A way, then, is a *constantly changing* state.

If the Tao is a way that is constantly changing, what is it exactly that constantly changes? The answer is: the conditions of *yang* and *yin* (more about these words in a moment). Let's not overlook something obvious about this. When something is constantly changing, it is in constant *motion*, isn't it? So really, we could say that motion is the way of the Tao.

Ki has the same characteristics as its parent, the Tao. Ki, then is motion like the Tao. Energy is motion. Energy is born from motion, and expresses itself as motion.

Now, what are these two states, known as yang and yin, which are in motion and are constantly changing into each other? In general terms:
Yang is the energy of an active state... outward radiation, thrusting, expanding, giving, the positive condition of light.
Yin is the energy of a passive state... inward absorption, yielding, contracting, receiving, the negative condition of dark.

Keep in mind that positive and negative, as they are used here, do not refer to a value judgment - one good, one bad. Positive and negative, as they are used here, are energetic states only. Candlelight flame, for instance, is a more yin-like fire condition than the blaze of a forest fire, which is a more yang-like condition. Neither is better or worse than the other; they are simply different manifestations of fire.

Ki, like its parent, the Tao, has the characteristics of these polar opposites, constantly changing from yang to yin, yin to yang, yang to yin, in ceaseless motion. And this "back and forth" motion is exactly what is known as oscillation or vibration. Ki vibrates!

Now we're ready to understand why ki has energy.

Ki Is Vibrational Motion

Anything that's vibrating in the back and forth motion of a wave - like ki - must do so at a certain frequency. Something can vibrate at a higher or lower frequency or anywhere in between, and different effects will be produced. When sound waves vibrate at a high frequency, for instance, we hear a high pitch; when they vibrate at a lower frequency, we hear a lower pitch.

Different ki vibrations produce different energetic effects, just as different sound vibrations produce different pitches. Again, looking at our language, we may say we are "high" energy or "low" energy, or "excited" or "brought down" - all of which are expressions referring to frequency. And we're certainly familiar with the energetic qualities belonging to these different states.

Different Energy States in Your Awareness

Why is it so important to know our energy vibrates at different speeds? Your human beingness is composed of different energy states, which we will discuss in the next chapter as different "bodies" which you possess. These different energy states are a result of your original ki vibrating at different speeds.

The fastest, most powerful vibrational state you possess is what I call your original Silent Master Consciousness. As this energy slows down in your awareness, it takes form as other energies which manifest as ideas, emotions, your physical body, and the material universe around you.

If it seems strange that you can have more than one energy state in your awareness, think of how ordinary water can exist in three energy states and still be water. Water is composed of the same elements whether it exists as a fluid, a gas, or a solid (ice). Of course, water can be in only one state at a time. Water cannot be liquid, gaseous, and frozen all at the same time. But you're different from water. Although the water's different energy states cannot exist simultaneously, yours can! Your different energy states do exist all together right now, and you can be aware of them all at once. You can be focused at the level of your Silent Master Consciousness and also be aware of your physicality, your emotions, certain ideas you are holding, and your environment, all at the same time.

This is, in fact, a very ideal accomplishment, and something to train for! We don't want to limit our awareness to just one energy state. Being stuck in just one energy state is clearly not an ideal situation, because you are cut off from other energies which can provide valuable input, intelligence, and guidance.

Unfortunately, sometimes we do get stuck in only one energy state, and this often leads to trouble.

Think of an instance where someone is caught up in anger. All he or she can feel is this raging, boiling, furious anger, and nothing else...Is this person able to take an intelligent action? Not likely. Might this person do something violent that would be deeply regretted later? It is possible. To alleviate that possibility, we need the training and discipline to keep all of our energies available all at once. Would you like to feel the benefits of being open to a more expanded state of awareness? It's available to you!

Ki Is Everywhere

The entire universe is a field of energy in motion. We've already discussed how something moving must do so at a certain frequency. Here's another thing to consider: something moving is in constant motion. Energy does not stay put. Energy is constantly interacting with other energy, and when this happens, it can change states. Energy can be modified to become stronger, weaker, more dispersed, more concentrated, faster, slower, all as a result of interaction.

Nothing is stationary anywhere in this universe. When physicists look at the tiniest pieces of matter, pieces tinier than atoms, and then pieces of those pieces, that which they see is in motion. When we look at the furthest reaches of the galaxy, as far away as we can see, that which we see is in motion. Everywhere in the universe, energy is moving. Energy is impacting energy, energy is interacting with energy, energy is changing energy. Even something "dead" is moving because its molecules are busy coming apart, its atoms flying into the air in the motion known as disintegration.

And all this energy is woven into one fabric, the fabric consisting of the original ki, which creates everything and sets it into motion.

You are one with this energy! It is present within you as your Silent Master. You are, then, one with the universe! You are connected to the galaxies, the sun, the fields of grass in Kentucky, and the mountains in the Himalayas in the sense that you share the energy that created those things.

You may ask: *If I am one with this universal fabric of energy, why do I not feel the snow on the mountain slopes in Tibet? Why do I not smell the flowers in Holland?* It is a matter of awareness only. The time may come when you have expanded your awareness enough to choose to do so...and you will do so.

There is a saying I have which I often tell my students: *There is no universe without you.* By this, I mean that the universe which you experience is as large as your perception. No bigger, no smaller. What you experience is what you perceive. The world you embrace is as large as your awareness.

One of my students, Stewart, worked at a large company here in the Silicon Valley. After about a year of training in Jung SuWon, he got a big surprise going to work one day. As he was walking toward the building's entrance, he suddenly saw a beautiful garden. He had passed it perhaps a thousand times, but never until this moment did he notice it. For him, the garden simply did not "exist." Through training however, his universe was expanding. He was becoming more aware of many things that had not existed until he recognized them: people that were available to interact with him, sports activities that he never knew he liked, musical talent which he didn't know he had, and now this garden which suddenly "appeared" one day.

Has something like this happened to you? How aware are you of what's around you? Are you wrapped up in a narrow, limited perspective, oblivious of special joys and pleasures than may be around you right now?

Many of my students who train here at the school tell me that at first they don't hear traffic or train noises outside. Then after some months of training, when their awareness begins expanding, they start noticing the noise outside as well as "new" sounds during their meditation periods. Let yourself open your awareness as wide as you can.

This universe is wonderful the way it is. We cannot invent any more riches in it. Everything that is, already exists. What we can do to enrich our lives is become more aware of what's already here! This means expanding our awareness of our entire energy field so that we embrace wider perceptions. If we see the world just in terms of physical or material energy and pursue only material goals, we cut ourselves off from dimensions that could enhance our joy and the adventure of being alive. The object of life is not just to exist. The object of life is to exist *meaningfully*, joyfully, energetically, purposefully, creatively!

To do that, we must develop and expand our energy, because we and the universe are made of many forms of energy. How do you like your universe? Are you ready to make it bigger? More beautiful? More fulfilling? More joyous? Dance with me, walk with me, let us sing together, and uncover all the beauty in the world around us. Are you ready? Let's go!!!

In the next chapter, we look at how our original ki transforms into the different energy states that make up our world of experience. This will be our first step in exploring and developing your natural ki energy.

Exercises

1. *Who Are You?* You are most likely well acquainted with yourself in terms of your occupation and your relationships. If asked, "Who are you?" you might say something like "I'm a mother," or "I'm an engineer," or "I'm a lawyer and a wife." Maybe these answers describe you to some extent, but be willing to consider they may not reflect your true or entire life purpose. Who are you really? If you believe you may not know your true self entirely, here's a way to begin getting in touch with undiscovered aspects of yourself.

Instead of analyzing the self you presently see in the mirror, imagine that you are creating a new "self," one that you paint or sculpt in your mind's eye. You are now an immensely creative artist...As you paint or sculpt yourself, what do you look like? What personality traits do you give to your "self?" What talents? What special abilities? What career? What kind of home? Where? What kind of relationships? Marriage? Friendships?

As you do this exercise, it is not merely wishful thinking. The creativity you are using to paint this new "self" is the very creativity your present self possesses. In this exercise you're giving yourself the freedom to explore your deepest inner desires and visualize them, and you can apply as many of these qualities as you can to yourself now, in whatever way appropriate.

2. *Look at your life as a patient and a doctor.* Very often, we are aware of a general feeling of discomfort, pain, or unhappiness, but we don't focus on precisely what the problem is. That's because we have a natural tendency to avoid pain. But you can help yourself only if you clearly define what is disturbing you, because only then can you take appropriate corrective action. So take a look now, and answer these four questions specifically. In this exercise you are both patient and doctor as you diagnose your problem and prescribe treatment.

a. What isn't working in your life?
b. What exactly is making the situation unworkable?
c. What would make the situation workable?
d. What can you do to manifest a workable situation?

Perhaps you've answered, "My marriage isn't working." And perhaps one of the items under "b." is, "My spouse will not resolve conflicts, and instead argues and nags without ever solving the problem." The response to this issue under "c." is fairly straightforward: "I/we need to have a more formal and finalizing way of working out problems." Responding to "d." may take much thought and effort. The solution will possibly require some willingness to change behavior patterns, to examine personality traits, to compromise, to be more sensitive to others, to accept new ideas. But find an action to take! Perhaps in this case the action is, "We could set specific appointments with each other where we will concentrate solely on resolving and finishing the conflict instead of fighting and arguing incessantly." If both people have a desire to reach a harmonious solution, then this method is an excellent opportunity to reach a successful resolution.

Meditation

*My Silent Master Consciousness
is within me now,
vibrating with radiance and bliss,
energizing my body, mind, and spirit with
life force and the colors of
pure, original Love
dancing through the universe right now.
I allow my pure Silent Master energy to
shine through my every thought, feeling, and action,
and this energy imparts grace, beauty,
purity, harmony, and vibrancy
to my words, my presence, my environment,
and every move I make.
I express my energy with balance,
allowing the changing yin and yang
conditions of my life to flow freely
from one to the other with serenity,
peace, and understanding.
Detached from the forms
I create and attract,
I am attached only to Love,
the energy
of my Silent Master Consciousness.
My awareness of this Love within grows
brighter and brighter with every moment I
accept myself as one with my
Silent Master.*

CHAPTER TWO

Ki and Your Body

I am infinite...
because my being,
my energy,
my dreams,
my joy,
shift and change,
shape and dissolve,
forever in unending motion.

Ki Forms Your Body

Recently, I was thrilled to watch one of my students, Mary, run and jump through the air over one of my instructors and kick a bag suspended from the ceiling the height of her head. Although this is a common exercise in one of my programs, it was a miraculous accomplishment for her. The room was charged and pulsing with energy.

Would you imagine that Mary was a young career woman who came to me with a severe case of rheumatoid arthritis a year earlier? At that time, her life, all activity, and her career were grinding to a halt in painful, physical deterioration. She had been on a whole string of drugs, including steroids, she had tried gold injections, and she had even tried some exotic experimental treatments. Yet the course of her disease marched steadily onward, becoming worse every day. Her body was weakening from lack of activity, and now doctors were talking about chemotherapy, which would have a further degenerative effect on her body. It looked like a full, happy, and active life was permanently over for Mary.

On the surface, it might seem that the physical demands of Jung SuWon training would irritate her condition even more. Yet after just a few weeks of Jung SuWon training, Mary began to straighten her contorted hands and actually press her palms together, something she hadn't been able to do for years! She still could not sit down or stand up without assistance, and she still moved extremely slowly within a very small range.

But there had been a positive response! Why? What was going on now that hadn't gone on before?

Your Ki Can Be Distorted

Remember, we discussed in the last chapter that Jung SuWon is energy training. Something was changing in Mary's energy. She was directing it differently, and this change was affecting her physical body in a positive way. To understand exactly what was changing, we need to look at her background.

Mary was a victim of sexual abuse at the age of ten. Her older brother was a fifteen-year-old who never learned healthy sexual attitudes because of his parents' inappropriate sexual behavior in the home. This brother coerced Mary and a younger brother, Mike, to engage in sexual relations, and no one - not parents, teachers, or friends - spotted this dysfunctional behavior or intervened. The effect of this incest over a period of years impacted Mary and Mike severely, though each in a different way.

Mike became withdrawn and uncommunicative and never allowed any sexual feelings to emerge when he reached puberty. He was so emotionally wounded by his brother's incest, he could not allow himself to feel sexual energy. But there is a big price to pay for repressing this powerful energy as it emerges: It becomes necessary to repress all feeling. This is the nature of emotional energy. If you decide to single out one feeling to suppress, you must suppress your entire capacity to feel, because all emotions are connected in one energy field. So to prevent sexual feelings from arising, Mike simply made himself numb.

As we discussed in the last chapter, emotional energy cannot be permanently dammed up this way. It eventually seeks an outlet, and in Mike's case, the outlet erupted violently in an attempted suicide. As fate would have it, the gun he used misfired. But sadly, a large part of Mike's being was already dead, and it was going to be a few more years before he would begin the process of recovery.

Mary formed a different response to the incest, although it was just as harmful. Her brother's sexual abuse taught her that her body was "not her own" to value, respect, and cherish, but rather belonged to him - or anyone - who wanted to use it. The incest taught her that she was not the one in control of her sexuality.

Of course, she also learned through this that her body was obviously "desirable." And this put Mary in a stance where she attempted to regain control in a negative way. She learned she could control others with her sexual desirability. In her teen years, she began engaging in indiscriminate sexual relationships with numerous boyfriends, all of which were understandably devoid of any genuine love or trust. On the one hand, she was merely demonstrating her lack of self-value in this behavior; but on the other hand, she was exercising control! She was the one in charge. She was the one who both attracted the relationships and ended them.

If you look closely at her behavior, you will see that it's actually a subtle form of withholding and contraction.

Like her brother Mike, the incest wounded her true sexual feelings such that she could not express them in a normal, valid, and healthy manner. Mike held back his true self and true feelings by suppressing them and going numb; but Mary held back her true self and true feelings by *distorting her energy* and putting on a promiscuous facade of control. In effect she was saying, *I cannot be who I really am, so I will hold in - or withhold - my true feelings, my true self, and be who I'm not.*

Consider the effect of this on her energy. This is like putting a dam in a free-flowing river. What happens as the water keeps flowing and keeps hitting the dam? The water accumulates on one side of the dam - the water is being *withheld* - and day by day the increased pressure on the dam weakens it until it breaks. The natural ki energy flowing through her joints, allowing her to bend and flex and move, is like a free-flowing river. Her joints should be like open banks for a free-flowing river, not a dam.

The decision to withhold or distort your true ki energy - as Mary did - is going to have the effect of a dam! In Mike's case, the dammed up energy erupted as an attempted suicide. In Mary's case, it appeared to be a psychosomatic contributor to her arthritis, a disease where the joints weaken and disintegrate like a dam on a river. You could clearly see the picture of Mary's contracted, withheld energy state when she could not stand up straight or stretch out her fingers and legs.

Yet, with Jung SuWon energy training, Mary's condition began to change. Why? Mary was willing to overcome her limitations.

Your Different Energies Are One Unit

Now we're starting to come to the main reason why I'm telling you this story. As I mentioned in the last chapter, your original ki energy manifests in four different energy states, which we can call your physical body, your emotional body, your mental body, and your spiritual body. Your original ki vibrates as the energy of matter, which is your physical body...as the energy of feeling and emotion, which is your emotional body...as the energy of ideas and concepts, which is your mental body...and as currents of light or electromagnetic energy, which is your spiritual body.

It is important to understand that these bodies exist together as one unit. That's why you experience yourself as having one body or one being! But these four bodies nevertheless each have their own characteristics and qualities. Even though these bodies are one unit, you *do* experience them differently. For instance, isn't it true that the *emotion* of anger feels very different from the *idea* of justice? And doesn't the feeling of your physical hand feel very different from an *electromagnetic* sensation of being "drained of energy"? If you want, and if you have excellent concentration, you can shift your focus so that you are aware *only* of the idea of justice, say, without feeling your hand or feeling drained. You can, with practice, shift your awareness to focus on only one of your bodies at a time. But you can also feel all these bodies at the same time. Isn't it true that you can think about the idea of justice (or lack of it) while feeling angry, feel the physical sensation of your hand holding something, and feel drained of energy - all at the same time? Your bodies exist all together, which is why you can experience them all together, all at once.

And now here's the point that relates to Mary's story: since all your bodies are different energy frequencies connected in one energy field, existing all at the same time, *they affect each other*. Remember, energy is always moving, always impacting other energies. Whatever you do in one body is going to have an effect sooner or later in your other bodies. This is why, like Mary, it's possible to strongly influence your sickness and to strongly influence your wellness. That is, you can use your own energy to impact your own energy! Would you like to learn how to do this better? You can!

Consciousness Shapes Your Energy

The withholding and negative control tactics which had been going on in Mary's emotional and mental bodies appeared as a manifestation in her physical body as arthritis. Since the energies of all your bodies are connected in one field, they will reach an "agreement" about your state of consciousness and manifest it. In Mary's situation, her overriding posture of withholding and control became "cast in stone," so to speak, and manifested not only in her emotional and mental bodies, but also in her physical body.

She began to get well with Jung SuWon training because she began to deal with and release the distorted emotional energy from the incest, and this released the effect in her physical body! Physical treatment alone was not curing her, because physical treatment was not addressing the problems in her other bodies which were being reflected in her physical body. All the medication applied to the physical symptoms but did not address the emotional factors.

The pain, contraction, and disintegration appearing in the picture of her arthritis were actually emotional/mental pain, contraction and disintegration. You may be wondering, *then why didn't she feel emotional/mental pain?* She did! But pain is painful. Nobody likes to feel it. So Mary, like many of us, looked for a way to escape from feeling it. And for her, sexual promiscuity and the illusion of control helped her escape from it. But as you can see, there is no real escape. Sticking your head in the sand doesn't make the world go away. Ignoring your negative energy does not make it go away. If you don't deal with it, it will faithfully show itself in your physical body eventually, one way or another.

If she had dealt with and removed the mental and emotional pain early on - instead of avoiding it - would that have prevented the onset of the disease? Possibly. You have to consider that even if Mary were genetically inclined to develop arthritis, as some people are, that doesn't mean she *automatically* would develop it. Two people can have the identical genetic propensity to develop a particular disease, and perhaps only one of them will. That's because there are many other factors besides just the physical factor that determine how and when or if a disease develops. However, since the mental/emotional factors in Mary's case proved to be the critical factors in her cure, we can reasonably assume they would have been critical factors in the prevention of her disease if she had dealt with them.

As Mary continued in the training, she got more in touch with her true self and her true feelings. And as her genuine energy began to emerge, she was able to discard the false self she had constructed and begin eliminating her controlling motives and attitudes. Then, when the negative energy of her false self began to dissolve, so did her arthritis, which was merely the picture of it! Of course, I don't mean to imply that everyone with arthritis has exactly the same background as Mary. But I am saying that a change in the picture of disease in one body will involve a change in the energy state of another body. Are you willing to begin practicing conscious control of your energy?

Become Aware of Your Four Bodies

Try this! You can do a few simple experiments to see how easily your bodies affect each other. Simply sitting in your arm chair, begin thinking about some situation that you considered unjust or unfair. Most of us have one of these stored away. This is your mental body in action, because obviously the events are no longer physical. They have passed in time and are now just mental constructions which you can remember and visualize. How long does it take before your emotional body responds with anger, grief, despair, sadness, or whatever? It may be quickly or it may take some time. But the point is, your emotional body responds automatically because its energy is connected to your mental energy.

Try the same type of experiment with a physical object. Take a piece of jewelry, for instance, or even a T-shirt or a shoe...hold it, look at it, feel it in an open, receptive, and quiet way...Undoubtedly one or more emotions will arise along with some purely mental constructs such as *Peter gave this to me on our first anniversary when I still loved him...or it was raining the day I bought this...* The physical object is connected to your other energies.

If you can, try slipping into some kind of feeling state right now. Maybe you're already in one, but if you're not, see if you can conjure up a feeling of gratitude towards someone. What *mental* ideas, memories, or concepts does this feeling arouse? What *physical* actions do you feel inclined to take as a result of feeling this emotion?

Have you ever had the experience of feeling terribly fatigued, and then after changing your environment or the people you're with, suddenly you revive? That can happen in just a few minutes time, which shows you how easily your energy can be affected by other energies.

The point I'm making again is that all energy is constantly in motion. The energy in one of your bodies impacts the energy of the others automatically. If you're sad or depressed, a "happy" action in your physical body - such as skipping or smiling - will impact your emotional and mental bodies and encourage them to respond with happy thoughts and feelings. If your physical body is tired, your mental and emotional bodies can communicate images and feelings associated with vitality. Meditations which stimulate your spiritual body can send a wave of recharging energy into all three of your other bodies.

Your original ki, then, transforms into these different energy states which we are calling your four bodies, and because they are all created from the same original energy, they are all connected and affect each other. Now let's zoom in on each of your bodies and explore their characteristics.

Your Physical Body - Earth

Many of the ancient traditions acknowledged that a human being has different energy states, which we are calling "bodies," but they also realized that humans experience all their energies on *earth*, not out in space somewhere. Earth is the place where we know we have these four bodies! Not surprisingly, then, some ancient traditions describe your four "bodies" with familiar earth elements: *earth, water, air,* and *fire.* These four elements correspond to the vibrational states of your four bodies. Your ki is not limited to just these four states. But since earth, water, air and fire are common and traditional ways to describe your human ki, let's look at this approach.

Your physical body is associated with the element earth, so we say that your physical body ki is *earth energy.* Earth is the physical place where you connect with everything else that exists, where you feel you belong to the life stream of the universe. When you say you feel "grounded," you mean you feel this connection. When your earth energy is healthy, you feel balanced, stable, with your "feet on the ground."

Just as the planet earth is the receptacle in which the other elements, water, air, and fire manifest, your physical body is a receptacle for your other energies: emotional, mental, and spiritual. Your earth energy, your physical body, is the center through which you balance yourself, express yourself, and feel your energies as a whole unit.

The planet earth is also made of the same original ki energy which created your physical body, so you can also consider your environment as part of your earth energy. As we discussed in the first chapter, nothing is truly man-made, because we simply arrange natural elements already in existence into new forms. So you can regard both your physical body and the material environment you live in as earth ki energy, and all your energies are connected to both.

Your earth energy is also your ability to nourish yourself. Just as the earth provides food which nourishes all creatures, you have earthly material work to provide nourishment for your survival. We refer to earth as "Mother Earth" precisely because earth is a bountiful giver, the ground source that gives birth not only to life forms, but also to the materials which nourish the life forms. When you express your "earthiness," you express your sensuality, your capacity to feel, appreciate, and participate with the objects made of earth.

Earth is the place where your physical being begins and ends. You are made of earth elements when you are born, and you return to earth elements when you die. Earth energy, then, is associated with *cycles* in your being, cycles of birth and death, sleep cycles, digestion cycles, breathing cycles, menstrual cycles, rhythms of activity and rest.

If your earth energy is not healthy, you are liable to feel nervous, flighty, disconnected, ungrounded, and experience your natural cycles out of step or unbalanced. When something is "unearthed" it is disconnected from the ground. So if you are unearthed, you are likely to be wandering in some fashion, unable to keep your thoughts, emotions, or physical actions on a fixed course. You may find yourself "infertile" in one way or another, unable to act as Mother Earth manifesting everything you need for the life you want.

In Chapter Three we will look in detail at the role of color vibration on your energy. For now, I will mention that each of these four elements is associated with a color vibration which resonates with the energy. The color associated with earth is yellow. When the earth energy is not healthy, this color may manifest in the skin or eyes as a signal that help is needed to strengthen the earth element.

Your physical body is the most dense of all your bodies, and certainly seems to be the most tangible. Of course it is tangible, and indeed, it is the flesh and blood material temple that houses all your energies. Yet, in another respect, your physical body is the least tangible.

Why? Because it is the most *impermanent* aspect of you. When it comes down to defining who you are, parts of your body can be "lost," for instance, and yet you still exist as a definable person. The aspects of you that are the most permanent, enduring, and significant in defining you as a person are your qualities of mind, feeling, and spirit.

Even if you had no arms or legs, even if you could not speak or hear, we would still know who you are because of your values, your love, your intelligence, your unselfishness, your motives, your intentions, and a host of other so-called intangible qualities. And even after you die, and you are no longer physically present, evidence of your intangible qualities may go on living a long time afterwards! Values that great men and women set in motion centuries ago - such as those framed in the United States Constitution - are still impacting us everyday. So truly, your physical being, although it feels solid and dense, is not the most tangible aspect of you.

In southern California recently, there was a massive fire that burned out of control covering thousands and thousands acres. During that time we all had an opportunity to experience the sense of loss with those who lost their homes and possessions, and to ask ourselves questions about where we place true value. Many people affected were interviewed on newscasts, and I was moved to see that even though people had thought material possessions were important prior to the fire, now because of this "opportunity" they were able to clearly see the things that are important in life. Sometimes, people had only a few minutes notice to get out of their home. What do you think was one of the most common items people made sure to escape with? Not the silver, not the jewelry...but photographs! Memories...irreplaceable photographs of moments of joy, moments of love, of victory, of togetherness...how incredible that these "intangible" memories of moments were so highly prized. But didn't this reflect their inner understanding that earth is indeed impermanent and that love is more tangible? Those people recognized that the precious moments of joy could last forever, with or without the photographs as reminders, and they also recognized that their ordinary material possessions could go up in smoke in a few seconds time.

But Earth's impermanence is not a cause for despair. Those same people who saved their photographs usually always commented with optimism that the house and everything in it could be replaced. That is the nature of something impermanent. It may go easily, but it also comes again.

Let us love our earth energy, and love the physical temple that holds our other energies. Let us take care of our temple and nourish it. We take care of our body with loving kindness, not because we are so attached to it, not because we are vain, and not because physical flaws or losses can prevent us from being "whole," but because our earth energy is deserving of great *respect as the center through which our energies express*. If a container is broken, it will not hold water no matter how pure, good, and "spiritual" the water is. Just so, our physical body is our container for all our energies. If we work hard to develop and purify our emotional, mental, and spiritual energies, let us work just as hard to have a body equal to the demand.

Your Emotional Body - Water

Your emotional body ki energy corresponds to the water element. Considering that our bodies are almost 80% water, it's not difficult to see the influence of this element in our lives. Our bodily fluids - blood, tears, saliva, glandular secretions, perspiration, excretory fluids - play a major role in our energy processing and are particularly responsive to our *emotional* energy. For example, think for a moment about how the emotion of fear impacts these fluids. Your adrenal glands secrete the fluid adrenaline to prepare your body for "fight or flight" so your heart beats faster, making your blood flow faster; the saliva in your mouth responds by drying up; you start perspiring; tears may flow; and in extreme cases of sudden fear, even your bladder control may be affected.

Water, which is fluid in essence, expresses the motion of "flow." Our bodily fluids are in a healthy state when they flow without obstruction or pollution. And it is the same with emotions. Like water, emotions are meant to flow unobstructed and without pollution. Just as water shifts and changes according to what it encounters, and then flows on, emotions have the capacity to shift according to the changing circumstances of your experience, and then move on. You can prevent this from happening, however, either consciously or unconsciously, by putting up emotional "blocks," which are ways to prevent yourself from discharging emotion. But the blocks you create will cause trouble of some kind.

Water can appear in unbalanced states such as flood and drought, and these have their emotional counterparts. We talk about *overflowing* emotion, *drowning* in despair, or being *flooded* with desire, and we also speak of dry lectures when there is no vibrant feeling, or being *washed up* or *dried up* when there is failure or a severe lack of motivational feeling. But water is also related to the energies of love, nurturing, and generosity which is where we get the expression the "waters of life." Think of how the Bible, for instance, refers to God, the giver of life, as the "spring of living water" (Jer. 7:17).

Since water's nature is to flow, the greatest hindrance to water or emotional energy is *blockage* of any kind. But even when we encounter obstacles, water teaches us the way to respond. The fluidity of water is what saves it from most situations of obstruction. Its fluid nature allows it to flow around, over, under, and sometimes *through* the obstacle. Even if there is an impenetrable block, often the weight, pressure, and force of water is sufficient to ultimately break the obstacle.

When we allow ourselves to feel emotion instead of trying to stop it, the energy will usually flow around, over, under, or even through the situation confronting us, just like water. The force of our expressed emotion may even dissolve the obstacle. You may be thinking, *but if I allow myself to feel my anger, won't I likely do something terrible?* You will most likely do something terrible if you don't express your anger and let it collect and build like water behind a dam. If you do that, your emotion will likely come out in an unpredictable manner with an unpredictable amount of force. It's far better to let your emotions flow through you in the present moment and dissolve their energy in the process.

What is the key to letting emotion flow? Love. Love in the sense of self-acceptance and life-acceptance. Your original ki energy can take on "colors" of feeling, everything from the dark emotions of hate and anger to the clear, bright and white light of love. But the original energy remains the same. So you don't want to cut off your negative emotions, because they are made of the same energy as positive emotions.

Love yourself enough to love *all* your emotions. The pure energy that created you also creates your emotions, so they are an aspect of you no matter what form they take.

Your efforts should not be directed to stopping the flow of emotion, but rather to changing the "color" of the emotion. You don't want to destroy your anger, for instance, you want to let it dissolve back into its original energy, love. But to change the

color of your emotions, you must first *accept them as they are.*
Think of emotions rising as bubbles arising in water. The
bubbles form, then pop back into their native substance, water.
When an emotion arises in you, it will automatically pop back
into its original energy if you let it flow through you and if you
don't suppress it or hold on to it fiercely.

Emotional "bubbles" are one way your energy communicates
with you. That is, emotions are loaded with information.
When you feel anger or jealousy, for instance, those emotions
are telling you something about your situation, maybe
something that you need to change or recognize. If you feel
anger or jealousy that your partner is turning his or her
attention to someone else, what is this anger or jealousy telling
you? What information is in these emotions? Are they telling
you deep down you don't feel "good enough" to have the
relationship? If so, you need to know this so you can do
something about it. Or are they telling you that perhaps you
or your partner are looking for relationships based on external
qualities like beauty or wealth rather than inner qualities? Or
are they telling you that maybe you need to be more aware of
his needs than you have been? Or are they telling you that
maybe you are overly dependent on having someone else's
attention and approval? What are the real reasons you're
feeling these emotions when your partner is turning away from
you? The information is very valuable!

So you don't want to pretend you don't feel the emotion or
try to make it go away. Instead, you want to embrace it and
learn all you can from it. This action you take of trying to
learn from the emotion helps to move the emotion into a
different and more positive form. Remember, energy does not
stay put. Emotional energy, like any other energy, is always in
motion, always changing.

When you have successfully learned from the emotion, it
will automatically turn back into its original energy, the
energy of love. The negative coloration dissolves when you get
the "information" from it and let it go. A passage from

Proverbs 3 in the Bible says: "Let love and faithfulness never leave you; bind them around your neck...Trust in the Lord with all your heart and lean not on your own understanding...This will bring health to your body and nourishment to your bones." This passage reminds us of how our original energy is pure love before we color it with our inferior or distorted motives and attitudes, and how it is healthy, pure energy in its original state.

We are "binding" love and faithfulness around our neck if we acknowledge that we can accept and transform the energy of negative emotions. Accepting our emotion means we trust the emotion will turn into the energy of our original ki, and that we are inviting the loving harmony of our ki to manifest. That's what is meant by "lean not on your *own* understanding." Our own understanding might tempt us to react to negative emotions, assign blame, make a big permanent reality out of negative emotion and become a victim of it...but if instead we know enough to release our negative emotions, we open ourselves to the harmonizing effect of our original ki.

And when we allow our negative emotions to dissolve into harmony, we invite healing of all kinds to take place. Our pure energy will reflect itself in a pure and healthy body. If, on the other hand, we allow certain prolonged emotional conditions to "get under our skin" like tumors, or "eat us up" like cancer, or "irritate" us like skin rashes, or if we find we can't "stomach" something or can't "swallow" something, we are making a place for those feelings to ultimately manifest as physical problems. It is much better to make a policy to allow our emotions to come and go like bubbles in water, learn from them, release them, and let them go.

The color which resonates with the water element is blue. When the water element is out of balance within a person, the skin may have a bluish cast, especially around the eyes, as a signal that this element needs to be acknowledged and strengthened.

Your Mental Body - Air

Your mental body ki energy corresponds to the element air. Breath or breathing is one of the most common metaphors in traditions all over the world to represent *life* or *life force*. In the Biblical account of creation, for instance, God "breathes" life into man. In the next chapter, we will look very closely at breathing, how it powerfully impacts all your bodies, and how you can use your breathing to maintain mental, emotional, and physical balance.

Certainly air is the most vital element for material life as we know it. You can live for some time without fluid (water element), without warmth (fire element) or without food (earth element). But how long can you live without air? A few minutes.

Air ki energy is the energy of your mental body, which is what you generally call your "mind." So we could say that air is the energy of *pure consciousness*. Right away we can see why air is such a vital element in human life. Everything that you are as a human being, everything that you experience, happens in your consciousness - your mind! You "know" that you exist because your "knowing" happens in consciousness. Just as you cannot have life without air, you cannot have experience without consciousness. Without this body of consciousness which we call your mental body, you would have no knowing of yourself, and therefore no experience of yourself. In fact, you process your awareness of all other energy manifestations, earth, fire, and water, through consciousness, your air ki energy.

Just as your emotional body forms its energy into feelings of different "color" and "tone," your mental body forms its energy into ideas of different types, some more constructive than others, some more harmonious than others.

You may have heard the expression, "thoughts are things." This is a way of expressing the concept that ideas act like seeds or patterns. You can think of ideas as blueprints which carry the information and energy to transform into physical/material objects, events or circumstances. Either way, the point is that the energy of your mental body ideas transforms into emotions and physical things, and these things take on the quality of the idea.

Notice that your air-element mental body, or mind, has a more spacious quality than your water-element emotional body. Air spreads out and fills all available space in an unconfined manner, but water, a denser substance than air, exists in a confined manner - like a lake, river, or ocean confined within its banks. Just so, ideas in your mental body spread out and cover all space just like air spreads out into space, whereas emotions are confined to individuals in particular circumstances, like water is confined to a place.

For instance, think about being in a room full of people. If you are feeling a particular emotion such as joy, it's possible you may be the only one experiencing that emotion at that time. Other individuals in the room could be feeling anger or grief or disappointment, and those emotions would be confined to them while your joy is confined to you.

On the other hand, while all of this is going on, the idea of, say, "chair," is present within *everyone's* consciousness. The idea "chair" is also outside the room where all of you are gathered. In fact, this idea "chair" is spread out everywhere in the universe, right now, available to anyone who wants to "think" it or use it.

Emotions and ideas then are very different types of energies and exist in a different manner. As we discussed at the beginning of this chapter, ideas and emotions - indeed, all energies - are connected in one field, work together, and impact each other. There is a constructive and a destructive way to use your ideas and emotions together. To illustrate, let's take a sample idea and follow it into manifestation.

Let's take the idea of "shelter." Most of us have no difficulty visualizing some manifestation of this idea, usually some kind of house. Clearly, shelter, as an idea, exists everywhere. We can make a shelter out of something as simple as a tree, or as complex as marble, granite, cement, wood, and bricks. A shelter can be a home or house, or it can be a little place around a campfire as it is for some wanderers, or an extensive range of land as it is for some ranchers.

Also, we can see that ideas usually involve other ideas in the creative process. That is, to turn the idea shelter into some kind of desirable manifestation, other ideas may also contribute and participate in the manifestation. Shelter involves ideas of self-acceptance (being "at home" with yourself), materials, beauty, togetherness, independence, recreation, rest, support, work, employment...we could make a very long list of all the ideas involved in shelter.

Let's say you want to manifest a home. You may say, "I want to have a beautiful home where I can experience feelings of peace, joy, optimism, and harmony, where I can work and play, which I can share with everyone I know." Then suppose you use your physical/material energy in some kind of action to actually search for a home, or improve the one you have. Now you are aligning your emotional, mental, and physical energies into one goal. Their combined energy, if unobstructed, will automatically work together in transforming into the energy of a material home, and you will manifest a house, apartment, or some other dwelling, depending on how you fine-tune your energetic work.

But suppose your mental body is holding concepts like, *I'm a bad person, I don't like who I am, it's selfish to want my own space, I can't support myself financially, I don't deserve to make a lot of money, nothing about me is valuable...* The energy of these concepts will impact your emotional body producing feelings of despair, depression, anger, resentment. If you think about it, many "homeless" people do indeed embody these very concepts. These energies will impact your material being, and you won't feel physically inclined to take any kind of positive action to procure a home. And in this situation, the combined energies of your mental, emotional, and physical bodies will transform into a material situation depicting lack instead of abundance.

If you try to hold both sets of ideas and emotions, they will combat each other, most likely producing a material picture where you're always "almost there" instead of being there. So it's important to use your energies in alignment with each other for the most powerful effects.

Think of alignment as purity. When you're trying to bring about changes in your life or manifest something, you need to make sure that there's nothing in one of your bodies that is polluting your efforts. If you believe you have your mental, emotional, and spiritual bodies all in alignment, but you don't take action, for instance, you are severely undermining yourself. When you find this happening, it's a signal to look at your other bodies for some kind of impurity. Is your mental body holding a belief in your "laziness"? If so, what in your emotional body is feeding this laziness? Feelings of inadequacy? Guilt?

One of the most powerful avenues of expression your mental body uses is your mouth: words! I always remember how the Bible says: "The good man brings good things out of the good stored up in his heart, and the evil man brings evil things out of the evil stored up in his heart. For out of the overflow of his heart his mouth speaks." (Luke 6:45.)

Consider for a moment how you "think." Don't you generally "hear" yourself think? You express your ideas in words, words which either play in your mind or words that you speak out loud. Words, then, have the power to shape the exact quality of your thoughts and ideas. Therefore, words have great creative power. We've all had the experience of saying something we don't mean, and finding that the words go right ahead and have an *effect*, maybe one we didn't want. It's very difficult to take words back!

Since words are the creative carriers of your mental energy, treat words with great respect and care! *Careful* means full of care. Choose words *carefully*. Think with them carefully. Send them out carefully to others. And be aware of the effect of other people's words before you "let them in." You don't have to accept every word that is spoken to you. Be aware of the mental intent in the energy of someone's words and decide if you will let it in or not.

The color that resonates with your mental body, air ki energy, is white. Just as white is the color which contains all color frequencies, your air ki energy - consciousness - contains your experience of all other energies. The purity of white expresses the pure, expansive nature of your mental body.

Your Spiritual Body - Fire

Fire is the element which corresponds to your pure life force energy, what I call the spiritual body. This energy manifests electrical or electromagnetic forces which operate just below the level of your physical body. This is the body of flowing energy which acupuncturists or acupressurists adjust in order to correct physical problems.

In a healthy state, this fire ki energy flows throughout the body in currents expressing the nature of yin and yang. In an unbalanced state, your physical body may manifest signs of too much yang fire energy (an excited, overactive state, such as a fever) or too much yin (a lethargic or stagnant state, such as a cold).

Acupuncturists have mapped the channels wherein this energy flows, and the pathways are connected to every organ, system, and subsystem in your body. There are pulses in your body which tell a trained acupuncturist where you have an imbalance in this flow of energy. When the area of imbalance is known, the acupuncturist can then insert needles in the appropriate channels to restore balance, and the balance will manifest as a healed physical body.

But acupuncture or acupressure is not the only way to work with the energy in your spiritual body. Since your spiritual body is electromagnetic energy, the electromagnetic energy in another person can also impact this body. This is where the "laying on of hands" comes into play as a healing technique. This energy can literally be transferred from one person to another through touch, or even through will power, because it moves around by following the laws of electromagnetic attraction and repulsion. That is its nature. A person in a healthy energetic state can bring an unhealthy person's energy up to a higher energy state and help them regain a balanced state. And conversely, if you aren't careful, a low energy person can bring you down to a lower energy state.

This energy is basic life force, the energy which gives you your aliveness, which is indicated by your *warmth*. A warm body is a *live* body, right? A dead body is cold. Life force, in its pure energetic state, is dynamic, sparkling, vibrant, enthusiastic, warm, the qualities we associate with fire.

And the other predominating quality of fire is light! Fire gives warmth *and light*. Light is the quality we associate with pure awareness or insight. Many cartoonists, for instance, use a little light bulb over their characters who suddenly have an idea.

A "fiery" personality expresses enthusiasm, which is the healthy, balanced state of the fire element! When this condition starts to get unbalanced we get either a "hot blooded" person, or a "cold fish," and either person is inclined to misuse their fire energy and act inappropriately.

Again, since all your bodies are connected, whatever you do with one will impact the others. Perhaps you are familiar with the practice of certain Buddhist monks who practice a meditation known as *Hwa Gi*, which is the *inner fire* meditation. In this practice, the monks focus so intently on their fire ki energy - which is what I'm calling the spiritual body - that their physical body literally manifests great heat. They can produce enough heat to dry wet sheets wrapped around them while they sit outside in winter snow.

On the other hand, in your emotional body, this fire is felt as emotional "warmth." The emotional quality of warmth is love. As I just mentioned, when these monks do the Hwa Gi meditation, the "fire" manifests in their physical body as heat. It manifests in their emotional body as feelings of great loving bliss. When we describe someone as "warm," we mean that person has qualities like kindness, caring, unselfishness, or generosity. Qualities which express love radiating outward to others - just like heat radiates outward. If someone is "all fired up" or "burning with desire" we are referring to similar emotional qualities of dynamic enthusiasm, appreciation, or zest for life. When a newscaster refers to a certain celebrity as being "hot," this is a fiery reference to the celebrity's expansive radiance.

In your mental body, we experience this fire ki energy as intelligence and will. When we refer to someone's exceptional intelligence, we say that person is "bright." We are also "sparked" by ideas, especially if they are "brilliant" ideas, all references to the light of fire. When a person devotes his will to pursuing some deep commitment, we say that person is a "firebrand" or is "on fire."

Since this body is pure life force energy, it feeds all your other bodies. It gives your other bodies their capacity to move, to be warm, to be alive, to transform. Your other bodies, in turn, mold this life force energy according to their special capabilities. Your physical body turns the energy into heat for physical activity; your emotional body turns the energy into warm feelings which "burn" and "glow" and "radiate"; your mental body turns this energy into ideas that "shine" such that you "see the light," or become "enlightened." Light and warmth, then, are the two basic qualities of this life force energy in your spiritual body.

Your sexual energy is driven by this body, of course, because the polarity of male and female is essentially a magnetic polarity. The fire ki energy of male and female polarities attracts naturally just like the north and south poles of a magnet! This is one of the reasons why you can feel sexual attraction or repulsion for someone you don't even know mentally or emotionally. The magnetic quality of this energy can act on its own, with or without input from your emotional and mental bodies.

Since this body is impacted by your other bodies so intensely, it responds to any and all activity in your other bodies. Therefore, meditations which focus on certain images, concepts, or ideas can profoundly affect the energy state of your life force. Certain images, for instance, will lead you to feel "charged," while others will just as quickly make you feel "drained," and all this can happen while sitting quietly in a chair, with the power of an image only. That's how easily your spiritual body responds to other energies. When we feel "influenced," "swayed," "overpowered," "attracted," "repelled," "induced," or "forced," these are situations where our electromagnetic energy has been affected by outside sources. In the next chapter, we will be looking at how to guard our energy so that we choose the energy state we desire, not just react as victims of the environment.

When your fire element is out of balance, you may feel a loss of sexual energy or an overabundance of that energy. You may experience inflammation, pain, or hot aching joints. Or you could experience poor digestion, heartburn, or poor circulation producing cold extremities or varicose veins and other circulatory problems.

The color associated with the fire element is red. Red flushing in the skin may be signaling an imbalance in this element.

Purity Is the Key to Harmony

The key to keeping all four bodies in alignment is keeping all four as *pure* as possible. Purity is simplicity. Purity is letting these bodies do what they're designed to do naturally, without interference, while supporting their functions with good habits.

For instance, you can honor and support your physical body

with good hygiene, appropriate exercise, and maintain a thoughtful, carefully evaluated diet. Everybody's body is different and has different preferences and needs for optimum performance. Be willing to consider your body as unique, and thoughtfully and carefully pay attention to the effect different foods have on your physical energy. Be willing to consider how fasting might help your physical body detoxify, and perhaps make some careful plans to experiment with different types of fasts.

You can honor and respect your emotional body by being honest, honest with yourself, and honest with others. If you think about it, any time you block your emotional energy from coming out, you're being dishonest in some way, aren't you?

I realize there are certain situations where you feel it's simply not practical to be honest - it will create an unnecessary conflict, or complicate the situation, or make things worse, or whatever - but there's *always a way* to be honest in spite of the potential problems. The honesty doesn't always have to be spoken out loud. Sometimes it's possible to be honest silently. If you can be honest about what you feel, and express it in *some* appropriate way, you won't be creating emotional blocks that will later show up as physical difficulties.

You can love and honor your mental body by giving it exercise...letting it be open to new learning, new pursuits, new goals. The more you learn, the more *capacity* for learning you create. It's as though your brain gets bigger with everything you learn, making room for more. A stagnant brain, on the other hand, seems to shrink, getting smaller and creating less room to hold new ideas.

Since your other bodies use the energy of your spiritual body to carry out their functions, you respect and honor your spiritual body by keeping your other bodies pure, including your environment and the people you allow in it. Your spiritual energy can be used by a negative thought or emotion as easily as by a positive thought or emotion. A willingness to meditate and seek the widest possible awareness will give you *insight* into the condition of your bodies; and you can then make adjustments and alterations as you desire.

The higher your view, the wider and more thorough your view. Think of viewing something from the ground, from the top of the building, from a helicopter, and finally from a satellite. Which gives you the widest view? The most information about the environment? The satellite, of course. The satellite view is like the view you seek when you meditate in one way or another. The information you gather in a meditative state gives you the highest, widest view, the insight you need to alter and adjust the energy of your different bodies. Try some of the meditation exercises at the end of this chapter.

Willingness to look, willingness to change, and willingness to persevere are the qualities which can save you from the effects of conflict and obstruction as you attempt to align your bodies, and work towards a certain goal.

In this chapter, we've looked at ways your physical, emotional, mental, and spiritual energy frequencies work together to create your life. In the next chapter, we will go one step further, and also look at how energy from your environment impacts you.

Are you now becoming more aware of how you exist as energy? You are as radiant, vibrant, flexible, and powerful as the original ki energy that created you. It is time to bring your pure, original ki into your life, and let it light up every part of your awareness with dynamic love and creativity!

Exercises

1. *Meditation*: Here is a simple meditation exercise that can relax your mind and help you experience more expanded states of awareness. The ordinary thinking process is so "noisy" that we rarely get a chance to experience other aspects of our consciousness unless we make a focused effort. (This exercise is not for while you're driving or in a situation where you need to pay attention to external matters.)

Sitting quietly, close your eyes and focus on your breathing. Begin to breathe rhythmically so that you inhale for four counts, hold your breath for four counts, exhale for four counts, and hold again for four counts. Gradually this entire process will slow down so that you are counting six, eight, ten, or more for each part. When your breathing is slow and relaxed, then just forget about it and breathe naturally.

Now turn your attention to your pure awareness. You will notice how thoughts come and go. Just "watch" these thoughts. Don't hold onto them, follow them, or fight them. Just let them come and go and flow naturally.

Eventually, you will feel your mind getting "clearer" as your thoughts slow down and simply settle like dirt in pond water. This clarity grows brighter as you practice this exercise on a regular basis, getting acquainted with who you are apart from your stream of thoughts.

This exercise helps you discover the purity and spaciousness of your Silent Master Consciousness as well as other states of consciousness you may not normally be aware of.

2. Make a point of observing how your different bodies respond to each other. When you're going about your daily routine, watch to see how your thoughts create emotional and physical effects or vice versa.

Meditation

*My Silent Master ki
is the energy of my real self,
energizing the fire of my spiritual body with the
power of pure life force...
shaping the earth of my physical body with
strength, beauty, and harmony...
stimulating the air of my mental body with purity
and clarity...
shining through the water of my emotional body
with love, grace, and compassion...
My bodies exist in harmony,
my energy flowing freely,
circulating peacefully without obstruction.
My four bodies work in unity,
each contributing the pure energy that expresses
my wholeness and completeness.*

CHAPTER THREE

Ki and Your Environment

I do not look
outside my Self
to know myself as you.
I move and I feel our colors,
I move and I hear our music,
I move and live in all our forms,
I move and I am the taste of our pear,
The fragrance of our magnolia,
The touch of our velvet, and
I joy at the sparkle of the facets in our
diamond.

Your Environment Is Made of Ki Energy

Your environment is as small as the rooms in your home and as big as the universe. Does it seem strange to think of your environment as being *made* of energy? As being *born* from energy? It's not so strange if you consider how your environment and everything in it came to be.

Look around you right now, and consider where the objects, structures, or landscapes you see came from. Whether you're in a forest, a Laundromat, or your living room, the composition of your surroundings began with primitive earth elements. Everything we build is a rearrangement of natural materials already in existence.

So where does earth and all its matter come from? Stars! Exploding stars, spewing out basic elements which recombine and take form as planets, earth, air, water, fire, all living things, all organic and non-organic forms. Earth, and all the elements of earth, living or non-living, spring from the same ki energy which creates stars.

This means your environment, and everything in it, is made of the same energy that takes form as stars and earth. Since everything in your environment is made - one way or another - from natural earth materials, we can say your environment is made of the original ki energy that produced the stars and the earth. Everything that exists is a form of ki energy.

And again, what is the nature of ki energy? As we discussed in Chapter One: *vibration*. This means everything around us is in motion, vibrating with a particular energy. We are vibrating with particular energies. So the energetic motion of our environment is constantly interacting with our personal energy. Why is this important to know? When motion interacts with motion, changes and alterations in the energy take place.

For instance, if a speeding baseball collides with a football in the air, the speed and energy of both will be changed. In a similar manner, when the energy of your environment interacts with your energy, alterations are produced that you may or may not notice, depending on your awareness. It's very much to your advantage, then, to be aware of what energy is around you so that you know what's affecting you and what's affecting your environment.

One aspect of my Jung SuWon training is to make my students aware of how to create environmental energy that supports them instead of hinders them. Let me give you a good example of how one of my students, Marla, dramatically improved her life by improving her environmental energy. You may find aspects of her story can help you assess your own environment and begin thinking about changes you can make to improve your life.

You and Your Environment Exchange Energy

A year before Marla started training with me, she had just been raped for the third time. Needless to say, many women experience enormous psychological trauma after even one instance of rape, often entering therapy or support groups for a good while afterwards. Marla went into therapy, but she continued to hold onto her trauma so tightly that she kept the "seed" alive, you might say. Remember, we discussed in the last chapter that ideas, concepts, and emotions are "blueprints" and can solidify in a material or physical way if held.

This is what happened to Marla. A second rape followed on the heels of the first, and of course, this intensified her fear, and it became even more difficult for her to release the imprint of rape from her mental and emotional bodies. And so, a third rape occurred, this time in her own apartment...The counseling that Marla underwent was not effective in removing her constant, ever-present fear and turmoil. Not a day passed where she didn't relive any or all of these rape scenes. And her distraught state of mind was severely undermining her ability to cope with the ordinary day-to-day stresses of life. I had to find a way to reach her and help her release this negative energy. As I wrote in my book, _Silent Master_, "Shock can mobilize your will." So I decided to try the following tactic to stimulate a reaction from her.

One day I asked her, "Were you raped last month?" She replied, "No, it was last year." I asked again, "Were you raped last week?" She answered, "No, the last time I was raped was a year ago." I repeated, "Were you raped yesterday?" "No, not yesterday!" she replied emphatically, wondering why I wasn't getting it. "It was last year." So I came right to the point: "Then why do you allow yourself to continue to be raped _every_ day?"

Being unable to let go of the mental and emotional images of the rapes, Marla was keeping the damage resulting from them alive. Although another part of her wanted to release this pattern and go on to a new happy life, she hadn't found the strength or the know-how to do this. The know-how in this instance was simply the ability to _forgive_. Marla needed to forgive her attackers - not because they didn't do anything wrong...they _did_...but because she could set herself _free_ this way. The act of forgiveness benefits the forgiving person greatly because it clears the body, mind, and emotions of negative energy.

It was clear to me that this victim pattern had solidified in Marla, and almost everything in her personal image and environment was reinforcing this pattern. Her wardrobe was drab and unflattering. She did not have a becoming hairstyle or use attractive makeup to emphasize her physical assets. She drove a car that never worked properly to a job that was boring and uninspiring. The decor of her apartment was oppressing and depressing and had not been changed since the rape occurred there.

I believed the road to recovery for Marla lay in uplifting her energy by completely changing the elements of her personal image and environment. The energy coming from objects of her past were literally stimulating the constant memory of the events of the past, and a new energetic environment was vitally important in stimulating a new mental and emotional outlook. I began working with her to change her hair color and select a wardrobe that was more vibrant and alive. This encouraged her to find a new, more gratifying job, and to buy a car that worked right. And, very importantly, she found a new apartment and created a decor with more colorful and exciting furnishings, an environment free of the image of the rape.

All of this happened with some resistance, however. The fear of change is something we all have to deal with, even when we desire a change for the better. Marla's old life was full of unpleasantness, but it was familiar. Somehow, for many of us, something unpleasant and *familiar* is more comfortable than the unknown and untried. Even though she was so unhappy and depressed that she had been pushed to the brink of suicide several times, she had become very attached to her material possessions - the very things that were keeping her a prisoner. But as Marla began making her transformation, gradually she let go of everything in the past and found herself a new person in a new environment, more assertive, more confident, more in charge of herself and her surroundings. It's simply a fact that when you want to create change, you must be brave and adventurous as you take charge of your life. Is it time for a new adventure in your life? This is the time to do it!

Your Environment Radiates Energy

Energy from our environment is impacting us all the time, but we can get so accustomed to the energetic quality of our surroundings that we aren't aware of its effect. You may have noticed that certain rooms in your home or other homes agree or disagree with you. You may have noticed there are certain stores and restaurants that affect you harmoniously or adversely. There are specific reasons why.

All the objects in any particular environment are made of energy, radiate energy, and *absorb* energy. After spending some time in a certain room, and finding our mood is changing, we will most likely say, "What's wrong with me?" The problem may be due to a particular energy from the room, and not something personal. For instance, furniture bears the energetic imprint of the person who crafted it as well as other owners or users of it. Have you noticed that sometimes you are attracted - or repelled - by a piece of furniture (or some other object) by "something" other than just its aesthetic value. You may find yourself saying, "I don't know why, but I just like this piece." Many times, you are responding to positive energy carried by the object.

When you go into a hotel, a restaurant, a store, or someone's home, you are being impacted by a whole range of energies coming not only from the persons, but also from all material objects. You can choose whether or not this energy will affect you if you are aware of it. If you aren't aware that there is certain energy in a particular environment, you will likely respond unconsciously, and find yourself with unexplained sensations. Of course, some environments can be uplifting, such as certain churches or ancient ruins, which reflect the energy of persons radiating positive spiritual energy.

The objects around you - your furnishings, your clothing - carry your energy, as well as the energy of others associated with these things. So it's important to clear away objects associated with past circumstances you are trying to change. When you surround yourself with paintings, photographs, or other works of art, you are surrounding yourself with the emotional, mental, and spiritual energy of the artist. So you need to choose carefully what you bring in to your field of awareness, because you are bringing in other energies besides just the material form.

Color Imparts Vibrational Energy

Color is a very powerful form of vibrational energy in our environment. We are impacted by color every waking minute in our home, office, supermarket, or any other commercial environment where someone wants to influence us.

What is color? We perceive different colors when we perceive light vibrating at different frequencies as it bounces off an object. Different colors, then, are different frequencies of light. Sunlight, or white light, is a mixture of many different frequencies.

As we discussed in Chapter One, when a wave - such as light - vibrates at different speeds, it produces different energies. So the different colors of the spectrum have different energies, red being the lowest, or slowest frequency, and violet being the highest, or fastest frequency. Since the energy of each color is different, each color will impact us differently.

We have already discussed how our original ki energy vibrates at different speeds to produce different bodies of awareness: physical, emotional, mental, and spiritual. Since we are made of vibrating energy, it's not surprising we are responsive to other forms of vibrating energy such as color, and it's not surprising that some colors are better than others in stimulating different aspects of our energy.

Every aspect of you is vibrating, even your skin boundary is not really a barrier. Your skin, eyes, and hands absorb color vibration and are affected by it, so the colors you wear, the colors of objects you *hold* receptively, and the colors you see do affect your overall energy. Disease, stress, fatigue, fear, anxiety...all these are disrupted vibrational states, and pure color vibration can help restore healthy vibrational balance.

Color has already found a therapeutic use in law enforcement and psychiatry. The color pink, for instance, has been found to reduce feelings of hostility and violent behavior. Pink walls or pink clothing are used for certain prisoners or psychiatric patients, as well as the cool, calming colors of green, blue, and violet.

If you're like most people, you have certain favorite colors. These are vibrations which harmonize with your general energy state. If you are bright and carefree, you will be attracted to colors like that. If you are quiet and passive, you will prefer colors like that. If certain colors resonate with unpleasant vibrational states you possess - like sadness, anxiety, or anger - you will describe those colors as "unpleasant" and avoid them. When you express your true, original energy, your Silent Master, you will attract your "true colors." These colors, your "best colors," will make you feel centered and serene because they resonate with your true energy.

For the sake of discussion, we can divide the spectrum of colors into two basic categories: the *warm* end of the spectrum, which includes red, orange and yellow; and the *cool* end of the spectrum, which includes blue, indigo, and violet. Green stands in the center of the two as having energetic qualities belonging to both the warm and cool colors. Green is stimulating like the warm colors in the sense of promoting vitality and healthy growth, but it is calming like the cool colors in the sense that it imparts a peaceful, harmonious, and balanced quality to growth.

I find it interesting that our planet abounds with the color of green, the color of peaceful, balanced growth. In fact, if you had 1,000 pennies which represented all the life forms on earth, only one penny would stand for earth life that isn't green based. Nature clearly likes this color of balance!

The essential difference between the warm and cool colors is this: Warm colors are stimulating and exciting energies; cool colors are calming and tranquilizing energies. Let's briefly go through the colors of the spectrum and look at the specific energetic qualities of each. You can absorb particular color vibrations by surrounding yourself with the color, whether it's

on the walls of your room, on your clothing, on objects which
you hold and look at, or in nature.

Red. Red stimulates and excites your nerves, pulse rate and
blood circulation, and lends energy to your entire system.
When you are fatigued, lethargic or sluggish for any reason,
red has an energizing influence. Red is vitalizing, but because
it is such a great stimulant it must be used with caution. Too
much red in the room makes the room look smaller, and may be
over-stimulating for long periods, producing feelings of anger
or irritation. A little red in your environment gives warmth, a
feeling of excitement and stimulation. Compassion, courage,
and persistence are positive qualities associated with red;
extreme passion and anger are more negative qualities. Food
which helps impart the red vibration to you are plums,
spinach, cherries, and radishes.

Orange. Orange has the same warming and stimulating
qualities of red, but to a lesser degree. It raises the pulse rate
but not the blood pressure. Orange strengthens your emotional
body, encouraging a general feeling of joy, well-being, and
cheerfulness. Lying between the red and yellow vibrations,
orange has an effect on both physical and intellectual vitality.
It has an anti-spasmodic effect which makes it a favorable
vibration for problems with muscle cramps. It helps remove
inhibitions, encouraging the mind to broaden and open to new
ideas. Positive qualities associated with orange are joviality,
self-assurance, and enthusiasm. A diet to fortify the orange
vibration in your systems includes oranges, tangerines,
apricots, mangoes, peaches, and carrots.

Yellow. Yellow is a very favorable vibration for mental or
intellectual activity, as it promotes a clear state of mind.
That's why it's very helpful for heightening your awareness
and alleviating depression, sadness, or any kind of
despondency. Our sunlight is essentially yellow. Consider how
beneficial sunlight feels when you need clarity or need to cheer
up. The yellow vibration, whether in the form of pure light or
yellow food, supports good digestion and elimination. When

decorating, remember that yellow, orange, and red, the warm colors, tend to make a room look smaller, but also perhaps cozier. Intelligence, intuition, optimism, and awareness are positive qualities associated with yellow. A diet to strengthen the yellow vibration includes pineapples, bananas, grapefruit, lemons, and corn.

Green. Green strongly influences the heart. As the middle color of the spectrum, the balance and harmony, green helps alleviate tension. When a diseased heart condition is due to an excitable nervous or emotional system, psychological or emotional disturbances, green helps restore a balanced state. It is particularly helpful after shock or a period of prolonged negative emotion. It imparts a feeling of renewal, freshness, and optimism. Positive qualities associated with green are generosity, humility, and cooperation. Foods which help impart the green vibration are all green fruits and vegetables.

Blue. To the extent that red is a stimulator, imparting heat (even fever and inflammation in extreme cases), blue is a tranquilizer, imparting coolness to your system. Red speeds up your system, blue slows it down so it can heal and mend. If you have been in an overexcited condition emotionally, mentally, or physically, the blue vibration encourages calm peace and quiet. Taken to the extreme, the blue vibration would produce the withdrawn stillness and quietude of "feeling blue," at which time the stimulation of red, "feeling rosy," is needed. Positive qualities associated with blue are willpower, aspiration, and reliability. Foods which help impart the blue vibration include grapes, blackberries, blue plums, and any other blue fruits or vegetables.

Indigo. Where there has been chronic depression or powerful negative emotion, even to the extent of mental illness, the indigo vibration has a reviving effect. Indigo has a purifying, stabilizing, cleansing effect when fear, repression, and obsessions have disturbed your mental body. It encourages your mental and emotional bodies to resonate harmoniously with your spiritual body. Isn't it interesting that purple is often associated with the attire of royalty? In the past, kings and other royal persons were expected by the common people to embody the spiritual qualities of a divine being. Integration, tolerance, and clear perception are positive qualities associated with indigo. Foods which support the blue and violet vibrations also support indigo.

Violet. Violet is the highest frequency, fastest vibrating color in our visible spectrum. So it is the *most* soothing, tranquilizing, and cooling color vibration. It stimulates you to experience the calm, peaceful, fluid harmony of your non-material energy states. Violet naturally promotes a meditational frame of mind, and encourages your emotional body to feel the spiritual bliss belonging to higher frequencies of your ki energy. Even more than indigo, it encourages the healing of unbalanced mental conditions in people who are overly nervous or high-strung. Idealism, dedication, and artistry are positive qualities associated with violet. Foods which enhance the violet vibration include purple broccoli, beetroot, and purple grapes.

White. When an object is white, it reflects all colors in the spectrum all at once. That's why you don't see a "color" when an object is white. So when your eyes and skin receive white, you are in effect receiving all colors. White is associated with purity because the entire spectrum is functioning in unity, with no one particular frequency standing out or predominating. White is a holistic color, bringing the vibrations of all frequencies to you all at once. White is a healing color, the color of choice in most medical or therapeutic institutions, because it contains any and all vibrational frequencies which a patient may need for recovery. Since white is a symbol of "allness," it is also a favorite color among religious groups. White is appropriate at weddings because the unity of male and female symbolizes the unity of allness. In Korea, white is worn at funerals as a symbolic recognition of the soul returning to the original energy that is the Source of all.

Black. Just as a white object reflects all colors of the spectrum, a black object absorbs all colors of the spectrum. Black is associated with power because all the vibrational energies of all colors are drawn into one place, ready to be used. But energy absorbed must turn into energy expressed. Wear black when you feel the need to draw energy to yourself for reviving your strength, energy, and will.

Paying attention to color is a way of expanding your awareness. Become consciously aware of how color affects you, and experiment freely. Treating yourself to beneficial color vibration is a way of caring for yourself and tending to your mental, emotional, and physical needs.

After you've had some practice experimenting with how different colors affect you, start making conscious decisions about how to use color in your environment. If you know that blue has a depressive effect, be sure not to buy a blue carpet no matter how well it matches. If you are forced to work in an office environment with a blue carpet, then you can make a point of surrounding yourself with other colors to counteract the blue effect. Wear colors that support your personal goals on any particular day. If you know you'll be meeting with a person who is emotionally volatile, it might be a good idea to wear white, for instance, and definitely avoid wearing red.

Also be aware of how advertisers and product packagers use color. Next time you're in the supermarket, notice what color combinations attract you, and decide if you're being "influenced" rather than making an aware choice. Notice your reaction to other people wearing certain colors, and again, determine if you are responding to vibrational energies of color rather than your own aware decisions about their presence or behavior.

Be Aware of the Power of Sound

Sound is another powerful vibrational source which impacts us every minute of every day. Sound comes to us in the form of conversation, music, and noise. Sound waves vibrate through the air and physically impact us. We hear because our ears have "equipment" that is designed to respond to vibration, but we don't need our ears only to experience sound. We've all had the experience of feeling loud music vibrations literally hitting our body.

Here's something you may not have considered: sound also impacts us through unspoken words, thoughts which we articulate through words in our mind. That is, there is such a thing as "inner sound," or silent sound, which affects our emotional, physical, and spiritual bodies as though it were external sound.

But first, what is external sound? A sound wave - the sound wave of traffic noise, for example - is a *package* of vibrations (any sound wave generally consists of many different waves superimposed on each other). When that vibrational package reaches us, our vibrating energy is affected by the particular energy of the sound package, and we experience a positive or negative reaction accordingly. If a particular sound is naturally "stimulating," we will consider the sound positive if we want the energy for increased activity, and negative if we want to sleep or be quiet. If the sound wave is non-stimulating or tranquilizing, like a lyrical flute, we will consider the sound positive if we want to be quiet, and negative if we want more energy.

But aside from our subjective feelings about what makes a sound pleasant or unpleasant, it's important to know that sound carries information besides just the physical sound. Sound is a "carrier wave" because it is something formed and expressed as a result of the emotional and mental intent of the sender. A simple way to see this principle in action is what we call "tone of voice." I can say the word "yes" many different ways with many different meanings depending on my intent.

But we can also see this principle in action other ways. A neutral sound, such as someone stacking books, may be annoying in one instance and practically unnoticeable in another, depending on the emotional and mental state of the person stacking. The sound will carry the emotional and mental information in that person's field at the time. This is also a reason why we like certain musicians better than others. It's not just their physical sound which we respond to, but also their emotional and mental qualities, which ride on their sound. For the same reason, we often find ourselves saying we prefer the quality in someone's voice over another person's voice.

Deaf people can also get information from sound by feeling vibrations in the floor or objects. Some use vibrations in balloons at concerts to feel the music. Sometimes they can "read" sound as effectively this way as the person who hears the audible sound. Animals also have their own way of "reading" sound. Think how some animals respond to subtle vibrations in the air and ground before a storm or earthquake. These vibrations are technically a sound wave. Although many animals pick up this information and act accordingly, these sounds are generally outside the range of human hearing and feeling. Only people with special vibrational sensitivity have been known to feel these vibrations.

Sound Is Creative

Sound functions the same way ideas do: as vibrational blueprints, patterns or seeds that affect how matter takes form. This is why the power of prayer, mantras, or chanting has been a formal practice in most religious traditions all over the world since ancient times. Your words, whether spoken or unspoken, do have power because they are *expressions* of the ideas and thoughts which move and shape the world around you. That is, when people pray or chant to bring rain, they are using the vibrational power of sound to make a vibrational change in their environment...in this case changing drought into rain. Certain American Indian tribes have been remarkably successful using this method to bring rain so vital to their crops and survival.

The practice of praying or chanting before eating in many traditions was more than an attempt to express gratitude. It was a way of imparting higher energy to the food, clearing it of negative energy before ingesting it. When you do this, you align your energies to take full advantage of the food. Since your food is ki energy, like every other manifestation in the universe, you can impact its vibrating energy with your emotional, mental, and spiritual intent - whether you express it through words like a prayer, a visualization of white light radiating from your food, or simply your "will" that the food bless, heal, and nourish. There are reasons why you prefer food prepared by certain individuals more than others, and some of the reason has to do with the quality of their energy field as they prepare it. Make an effort to prepare your food with healthy energy!

The words that you think and say as an individual, as well as the words you share in common with some larger group, have an effect on your energy, the energy of your collective environment, and of course, the circumstances and events which you create with those words. How important it is, then, to watch your words, to select them carefully, and to guard against putting out "sounds" which are destructive or inharmonious. When words are shared with a group, the vibrational power takes on a force proportionate to the size of the group. That's one reason why group efforts are often more successful than individual efforts in bringing about some big change or transformation.

There's a saying I give to my students because I know how important it is to their well-being: "Guard your mouth." Your mouth is a powerful instrument of sound and has enormous power to help or hinder you in your dealings with other people, in fulfilling or obstructing the goals you set, and in directing your energy appropriately in meeting the many challenges of everyday life. This is something you can do right now. There's nothing to stop you from watching your own mouth and thoughts!

What Is Your Inner Sound Creating?

Many of us carry on an unspoken inner monologue constantly that reflects our opinion of ourselves and the environment. Take a good look at those words that play in your mind as your inner voice does your thinking and feeling...Are they words you want to see take form as events, circumstances, places, people, or things? Always remember that these inner words are vibrational blueprints which will tend to "solidify" into actual physical experience. You do, indeed, have to take responsibility for your words, because they do have power.

You may believe that "what you think" doesn't matter, only what you actually say or do. Not so. Again, your thoughts are *words*, and your words are patterns which take form. Sitting around thinking strongly of how much you hate this certain person, with an inner monologue filled with statements of revenge...all this will simply create a cloud of negative energy around you that will probably attract these things you're thinking to you! The other person's brighter energy state will most likely protect him or her from your ill will, and you will be the unhappy victim of such negative thinking.

Listen to your inner words. Frequently check to make sure you're talking positively about yourself. If you find a monologue running that goes...*I'll never make it...I'm no good...nobody wants me...nobody values me...I have nothing to offer*...on and on...then you need to consciously stop and consciously create new words. *I am succeeding...My talent is valuable and desirable...I have my unique contribution to make...I am attractive*...whatever you need to say to help you on your way, not hinder you.

Are Your Five Senses Friends or Foes?

The way you are aware of the energy in your environment is through your five senses. Your eyes, ears, nose, mouth and skin are all communicators of energy, both receiving it and sending it.

I sometimes refer to your five senses as five "thieves" because, if you're not careful, they can rob you of the positive impressions you should have. When you *see* and *hear* discord in the office coming your way, what do you most often do? Do you allow the energetic sensory impressions you're receiving to go unchallenged in your own mind, and simply accept the situation of being robbed of peace? Or do you make a point of consciously sending out energy, words, and actions which reflect a more peaceful energy? If you do the former, you're allowing your sense of sight and hearing to rob you of the harmony which is rightfully yours. If you do the latter, you're allowing your senses to perform a valid function: namely, give you information so that you can make a conscious decision about how to direct your energy.

If you don't want your five senses to rob you of your natural harmony, use them as friendly communicators, giving you the information you need to adjust and direct your energy. Always seek the highest and best experience you can with your five senses, and don't settle for discord without challenging it. Demand that your five senses seek out and express your true, pure energy.

High Energy Transforms Low Energy

Everything around you is made of some kind of energy. What is the difference between true, pure energy and distorted energy? The difference is like that between music and harsh noise. True energy produces harmony and peace; distorted energy produces discord and disharmony.

But again, energy is energy whether it appears in a pure state or a distorted state. When you feel that wonderful sense of warm love, for instance, you're feeling your true energy. When you feel that discordant feeling of bitter hate, it's that same love energy distorted, colored with particular beliefs and ideas that darken your natural bright love energy.

Generally speaking, true, pure energy is a "higher" vibration than the distortions of it. Warm love is a higher vibration than bitter hate. Perhaps you are familiar with the concept of *entrainment*. Entrainment refers to the tendency for a stronger, faster vibration to affect a nearby slower vibration. What is the effect? The faster vibration tends to bring the slower vibration "up to speed" until both vibrations are moving at the same frequency. If you are in a situation of discord, your "high frequency" love energy can "entrain" the lower distorted hate energy, causing it to come up to speed, and transform back into its original high frequency love. That's why love heals. The energy of love in a discordant situation can transform that situation!

So again, if you use your five senses to bring you information instead of letting them rob you of peace, you can consciously choose to impact any given situation with your own "higher" energy, and bring about healing, resolution, and transformation wherever you are.

Discord is simply a distortion of true energy and can be corrected by sending out the higher, true energy. Irritability is a distortion of pure, natural serenity; selfishness is a distortion of pure, original generosity; destructive competition is a distortion of the pure energy of harmonious cooperation. You can make the choice to reflect the genuine energy states and dissolve the distorted states in the process.

What happens if you don't do this? You simply find your energy drops to the prevailing status quo. The presence of low energy has a "draining" effect on a high energy source such as a healthy, vibrant, radiating person - *unless* that high energy source consciously guards against being drained. This means if you are a healthy, vibrant, radiating person and you want to stay that way, you must be aware of the aggressive low energy states around you and dissolve them! This doesn't mean you go around like an energy policeman looking for trouble to correct. It just means you maintain a state of awareness so that you always know what's going on around you.

Guard Your Energy State

Energy has a "sticky" quality. If you aren't aware of the energy states around you, you will likely pick up undesirable energy without even noticing. Have you had the experience of feeling good, then spending some time around a depressed person? Did you later experience that your cheerful mood just vanished, and that you were now feeling depressed yourself? This can't happen if you simply make yourself consciously aware of the person's state, and make a point of continuing to emanate your own higher energy of love and well-being.

Another way we pick up energy is through the media, which bombards us with all kinds of subliminal colors, sounds, ideas, and messages. When you're watching television, do you consciously analyze every commercial as to how color, words, music, and images are deliberately manipulating you? Probably not. Most of us just don't give television commercials that kind of conscious attention. Even if we withhold our conscious attention, our subconscious mind still receives everything that is heard and seen. So we can pick up the energy and intent of advertisers just by being exposed to it, just by having it in our field of perception. Many of those fast food commercials are designed to make you hungry - even if you're not - and they very often succeed unless you are aware of how you're being manipulated.

Protecting yourself from picking up undesirable energy takes practice. One of my students, Beth, came from a discordant family where there was arguing, alcoholism, lying, and conflict going on almost all of the time among the two parents and three children. After moving away from the family and entering Jung SuWon training, Beth began to feel much higher energy states, even to the point of it having a curing affect on her chronic inflamed skin condition. When there was a death in the family, she had to return to that environment, and she didn't consider her visit any kind of problem.

Right away, she discovered the training had made her much more sensitive to energy states around her, and the discordant family environment was almost unbearable to her at first. But slowly, as the days passed, she found herself blending in more and more to the family scene, even participating in some of the arguments and taking a drink here and there to dull the pain. At the end of five days, she was feeling comfortably "dead," as she put it, no longer feeling so assaulted by the environment. But her skin erupted again.

Beth had not learned enough about protecting herself to go into an environment like that without being harmed energetically. A higher energy state will drop, as it did for her, unless you consciously maintain it with awareness. If you do maintain it, then your high energy will most likely entrain the vibrational energy around you instead of dropping to a lower energetic level. Even if those low energy persons consciously resist you, you can still at least protect *yourself* by maintaining your high energy.

Use Breathing to Control Your Energy States

The more pure and true your energy is, the more you are protected from the harmful effects of negative, distorted energy states around you. As we've just discussed, however, the challenge is to maintain your high energy state even when you are "under siege."

One way to both protect your energy and control it is through breathing. Your breath, including your breathing style and breathing patterns, is the prime mover of your ki energy.

You may have already noticed that your breathing changes in different emotional states. When you are calm and relaxed, your breathing is slow and deep, and most likely your abdomen is expanding with your inhalation and contracting with your exhalation. If you are nervous, excited, or frightened, you take quick shallow breaths and your chest is expanding and contracting - not your abdomen. In extreme cases of fear, some people hyperventilate. In extreme cases of depression, the lack of oxygen from shallow breathing increases the sense of lethargy and dull thinking. You can be trained to use your breathing to alleviate pain, as in childbirth, and to change your emotional state.

Before talking about the most optimum way to breathe for enhanced relaxation, centeredness, peace, and poise, let's look at stressed breathing patterns.

When you are frightened, highly stressed, or very angry, your body goes into "fight or flight" mode, an automatic response in your nervous system that increases heart rate, blood flow, and adrenaline. Your blood flow is diverted to muscles for movement, and the liver is stimulated to provide more blood sugar for quick energy. Nature understands that you don't need your energy in the abdominal area for digesting food at this time, so the abdomen tightens. Part of the tightening is also due to your instinct to protect your essential organs in that area. As a result, in this "dangerous" situation, you cannot breathe deeply because your diaphragm, which normally moves downward with a deep breath, cannot budge against the tight abdominal muscles. So your breathing motion goes up into your chest, where you are forced to take short, rapid breaths.

All of this is an automatic response which occurs when you are in danger. The problem is, the stresses of modern life force us to live in a "fight or flight" mode much of the time. We don't have wild animals to confront, but we do have to confront an angry boss, for instance, or aggressive and aggravating drivers on the freeway, and this is enough to create the "fight or flight" syndrome. Even though this pattern is an automatic response, we get locked into the breathing pattern on a more or less permanent basis. What happens next is that the breathing pattern itself becomes a cause for a sense of anxiety, and then the resulting anxiety goes on to reinforce the shallow breathing. In short, a vicious cycle is set up where the breathing causes the anxiety which causes the breathing, on and on...Next time you're out shopping, take a look at the people you encounter in stores, restaurants, or wherever. You'll probably notice that most of them are breathing from their chest area. This is a chronic and pervasive problem in modern life.

The way out of this automatic vicious cycle is to breathe with conscious awareness, allowing the abdomen to expand and contract with each breath. This is the way nature intended the respiratory process to work under normal circumstances. Even when you are in a situation that is not "normal" - such as great fear or stress - you can still breathe this way to reduce anxious, frightened feelings.

There is a center two inches below your navel called the Tan Jun. In many oriental meditation traditions, the practice of breathing into this area is praised for bringing spiritual growth, warmth, and a *greatly enhanced sense of peace and well-being*. Clearly, these practices are based on the understanding of the power of optimum breathing.

The next time you are very stressed, frightened, anxious, or depressed, try this. Sit comfortably or lie down on your back. Put your tongue against the roof of your mouth and breathe in through your nose. Imagine that the air is light, and imagine that the light travels from your nose, down your wind pipe, into your lungs, and then keeps on going out the bottom of your lungs, pushing your diaphragm down, and then finally comes to rest in the Tan Jun two inches below your navel. Your abdomen must expand into a rounded state to do this. Hold your breath there as long as you can without strain. Then slowly, slowly, breathe out through your relaxed mouth, letting the "light" remain at that spot where you directed it. Your abdomen will naturally contract.

As you do this four or five times, you will begin to feel your physical, emotional, mental, and spiritual bodies respond to this loving energy. You will calm down, you may begin to warm up, and you may begin to feel some of the bliss this energy carries naturally. Breathe this way as long as you need or want to, and make a point of keeping your breath moving this way no matter what situation arises, no matter how stressful. This way you remain in charge of your body and in charge of making an intelligent, aware response to the situation instead of an automatic reaction.

You can also do this breathing for a certain physical problem. Let's say you have a pain in your hip. Instead of breathing your light into your Tan Jun, breathe it into the pain. After you've done this for a while, maybe a few minutes, maybe a few days, don't be surprised if you suddenly experience an emotional release, followed by an alleviation of the pain. This manner of breathing is very effective at dissolving mental or emotional blocks which have "solidified" in your physical body.

Use Meditation to Protect Your Energy

Meditation, whether you do it formally or informally, is a way of seeking purer states of consciousness, actively seeking the true, original Consciousness of your Silent Master. In _Seven Steps to Inner Power_, I give a basic meditation for beginners, a formal meditational exercise designed to lead you to an awareness of your Silent Master.

But right now, I'd like to stress an informal type of meditation you can do all day long, every day, to guard the quality of your energy. And it is: _watch_! Even though you have an inner monologue going on most of the time in your mind, and even _while_ it's going on, there is another part of you we can call your "inner eyes," which watches your inner monologue and listens to it! Naturally, this is a very objective part of you. Your inner eyes do not speak like your inner voice does, because they are busy _observing_ your mind, including your inner voice.

Why are your inner eyes so important? When energy is moving around - as it does from person to person and back and forth between you and your environment - it will latch onto you unless you see it coming. Most of the time when you find yourself angry, or depressed, or anxious, or whatever, there was a moment when that energy impacted your field and changed it. But you didn't notice this exact moment, and instead you found yourself declaring, *I'm mad* or *I'm sad*. At this point, the energy is much more difficult to transform than it would have been earlier. At this point you've already accepted it and it's already got you off balance.

If your watcher is turned on and working, however, you will see the exact moment this negative energy hits your field. That's the time to eliminate it! Right there.

It doesn't matter whether the energy is coming from outside you or from within you. Anger, anxiety, depression, resentment, jealousy...any and all negative energy is far easier to dissolve and transform at the moment of impact. And you can be aware of this moment. In fact, it's very interesting to experience anger at the very moment it hits you. If your inner eyes spot it, you'll feel how "alien" it is to your whole being, and how unpleasant and how undesirable. But if you simply become angry with no awareness of when it happens, the anger feels much more a part of you, and that's why it's harder to get rid of it at that stage.

I will warn you right now that this simple exercise is possibly one of the most difficult tasks you will ever undertake. Our minds, as a rule, are not at all sufficiently disciplined to carry out this practice every minute of every day. You will be lucky if you can manage it for a sum totaling thirty minutes daily. But I strongly urge you to start working on it, because it can totally change the way you handle your energy. And, as I hope I've expressed in this chapter, handling your ki energy more effectively is the key to changing your life! Everything is energy. You are energy. You environment is energy. Learning to watch your energy, guarding and valuing it with loving care, is worth every effort you can make!

Exercises

1. *Inner Eyes Meditation*. This exercise goes one step further than the exercise at the end of Chapter Two. As described in that exercise, sit quietly and slow your breathing down as much as you can. When you feel calm and relaxed, forget about your breathing and turn your attention to your pure awareness. With your inner eyes, begin watching the empty space in your mind. As soon as you perceive a thought arising, count "one." Notice that the thought will pop like a bubble. As soon as the next thought, feeling, or image arises, count "two." Continue on and on like this for about fifteen minutes. This exercise drives home how thoughts, feelings, and images are simply bubbles of consciousness that arise spontaneously and vanish into empty space if not pursued. The more you practice, the more easily you can create a calm and tranquil mind space, and this frees you to experience higher, wider, more expanded states of consciousness. Also, this practice helps you gain more control over what thoughts you will or won't allow into your mind space, and this results in more self-control and personal power.

2. Try this same exercise in an informal manner as well. When you can't sit down in a formal meditation described above, try this same exercise while putting on makeup, shaving, folding laundry or doing the dishes - but not while driving, of course.

Meditation

My Silent Master Consciousness
and I
are one,
my awareness vibrating in unison
with pure, original, creative ki.
I allow the love, peace, bliss, and serenity
of my Silent Master
to express through my body, my senses,
and in everything I create as my environment.
My Silent Master Consciousness
looks through my eyes
to value all the colors of love in earth's
shapes and forms;
listens through my ears
to create sounds
of harmony in every environment,
in work and play, in quiet and celebration;
senses through my nose to appreciate the unique
fragrances of all life forms;
reaches out with my touch
to feel the oneness of all creation,
all earth's children;
speaks through my mouth to impart words of
blessing and healing everywhere I am present.

CHAPTER FOUR

Ki and Relationships

True lovers are we,
I and my creation...
Exchanging our passion in a
Universe of color and sound and heartbeats.
I give Light to my creation
and speak of fiery Love.
My creation reflects Life back to me
and speaks of devotion.

Relationships Form With Shared Energy

One common complaint I hear frequently from everyone is their difficulty with relationships - spouses, friends, co-workers, relatives, in-laws, neighbors, and everyone else. How can we get along better with others? Why is there so much difficulty in getting along with others? Why isn't it easier to solve relationship problems? Often, unresolved relationship problems go on and on for years and sometimes never get worked out.

Although we sometimes talk about relationship problems as though they are a modern issue, let's not forget that relationships have been around since the beginning of humanity. We don't live alone in this world, we have never existed alone, and relationships are necessarily a part of every aspect of life.

Nevertheless, we experience ourselves mainly through our sense of being an individual. But ironically, one of the things that strongly defines our unique individuality is the fact that we exist *in relationship* to others. By that I mean, one of the main reasons we strongly feel our "self" is because we know "others." These opposites help define each other!

In this chapter we're going to look at how our energy impacts relationships. It seems that relationships are composed of two entirely separate forces: the energy of our "self" and the energy of the "other," whoever it may be. In general, we regard these two forces as completely independent actors.

While it is true that every person is responsible for their own behavior, it's also true that the energy of "self" and "other" operates in a *unity*. When you say, *I'm not responsible for that person's actions...or I'm not responsible for what you did or didn't do to me...* that's true, but it's not the *whole* picture. This is a narrow view which does not take into account the very important fact right here: Your "self" and "other" are *strongly connected* in a unified energy exchange even though each do indeed have responsibility for their own actions.

You can refuse to embrace this larger picture, of course, and stick rigidly to the idea that you "have nothing to do" with the other person's actions or presence in your life. But you are greatly disadvantaged when it comes to successfully *eliminating* conflict, hostility, blame, and vengeance, and other ills that plague your relationships. Why?

In order to resolve relationship difficulties, we have to understand two things: first, how we helped create or attract the energy that the "other" is manifesting; and second, how we can correctly use our own energy to create or attract a better kind of "other."

Your Silent Master Relationship

Just a moment ago, I mentioned that we have "never existed alone." Don't forget, the moment you are conceived, you're in a relationship. You wouldn't have arrived here at all if it hadn't been for the relationship with your mother in her womb. Then, after you're born, you are in a relationship with family members. From there, your relationships continue to expand as you find yourself in relationships with larger and larger communities.

But you also have a relationship with the life force that created the universe! You had this relationship before the one with your mother, before you were born, and you still have it now. If, as you're growing, you're also growing spiritually, you will ultimately approach your Silent Master Consciousness and regain a wide-awake awareness of your connection - to your relationship with the entire universe! This is your first original relationship from which all others follow, one that will never end. My fourth Silent Master Image (in my book *Seven Steps to Inner Power*) says:

IV

YOU ARE CREATIVE ENERGY

Your Silent Master knows Itself as
the Source of mental, emotional, and
material Energy - your Energy, which
you are free to utilize and creating
what you desire. Therefore, you are a
Co-Creator, cooperating with the
Life Force of the Universe to shape
yourself and the world around you.

This Image tells us that when you become aware of your
Silent Master power within you, you feel at one with the entire
universe, aware that you are connected to all life, all light -
with a love that embraces everyone and everything in the
universe. Yes, this is a very wide consciousness, a very *wide*
relationship, much wider than your narrow, egotistic, strictly
materialistic personality concerns. But your Silent Master
Consciousness exists for you to discover! My goal in giving my
Jung SuWon training is to help and encourage my students to
reach for this inner power, peace, freedom, and joy.

This Silent Master Image also reminds you of your
unlimited ability to creatively manifest your dreams in the
entire universal field, part of which is our earth here and now.
You have a relationship with this universal field because you
are one with it! So everything in the universe is available to
you to the extent you *become aware* of it. You cannot manifest
what you're not aware of in some way.

Remember, when you wish to create or manifest any aspect
of your life, you do not have to invent anything. All you have
to do is open your awareness wider and wider, and your infinite
capabilities and richness will become more and more *visible*.
Jung SuWon does not teach you something new. It teaches
what you already have - what you can open to as you become
more aware.

You have, then, a relationship with the universe that is infinitely open, full of unlimited, as yet undiscovered potential. But now, since we are on earth at this point in time, let's go back to your first earth relationships with your mother and family. These are important relationships which go on to affect every other one you have for the rest of your life. It's important to be as fully aware as possible of the concepts you formed at this time. Would you really like to improve the quality of your relationships right now? There is a way to do it, and it begins by looking very carefully at your first relationships!

Early Relationships Create Repeating Patterns

Your very first impressions about who you are, what you're like, and what you can do with your abilities come from your first relationships. I know of very few people who were born into ideal family circumstances. Some people I know were born into situations where many negative family-taught beliefs - or cultural beliefs - effected them in a way that made it difficult for them to find their true self. I was born into a family and a culture where there was much to overcome in order to fulfill my true desires. In a moment, I will share some of my background with you to discuss some ideas about how upbringing affects future relationships.

Why do we look at our upbringing to analyze the quality of our relationships? You must identify if there were negative or alien energy patterns you adopted from your first relationships, because these patterns will tend to *manifest* in all other relationships. Or, put it this way: you must identify and express your true self to attract harmonious relationships.

Why do the initial patterns we adopt go on manifesting over and over? Because the patterns have energy, and this energy follows the rule of "like attracts like." What we're talking about here is *resonance*. Resonance refers to the fact that a particular vibration will arouse a like vibration in something nearby. For instance, the vibrational frequency put out by an airplane flying over your house *resonates* in your window, and your window vibrates in sync with that frequency. Your living room couch most likely does not resonate with the airplane's frequency. Why? Resonance can occur only when there is a *receptivity* to the vibration. The window is receptive; your couch isn't.

In a similar manner, your energy - your patterns of energy - will resonate in those persons who have similar energy and who are therefore receptive. People with resonating energy tend to form relationships because the resonance is felt as a stimulation and attraction. That's where the expression "like attracts like" comes from. A like vibration arouses, and attracts, a like vibration in others.

So the first step in cleaning up your relationships is to take a good look at the traits you may have adopted in your early relationships. The next step is to look at how these traits or patterns are being repeated right now in present relationships. Identifying these traits or patterns gives you something to work with. Once you know what you have to overcome, you are in a position to do it. Since I don't know your specific upbringing, I will share mine with you. Mine is certainly filled with the ills and pitfalls that some people experience one way or another. First I'll give you an idea of what enabled me to overcome my obstacles; then we'll look at the other side, at what feeds obstacles and causes them to manifest in relationships over and over (until you change your energy).

Family Abuse and Discrimination

The life I have now was certainly not inherited! In order to create the life I truly desired, it was necessary to overcome a family and culture that denied me what I wanted out of life. If you have similar struggles, hopefully my victory over my environment will encourage you to believe in your true self and your ability to bring out the life you desire.

When I was born in Korea, nobody rolled out the welcome mat! I was born *female*, my first obstacle. In the oriental culture at that time, women were cast in a role which nobody questioned. Women were trained to cook and sew and were not allowed to have expectations beyond being a good wife and mother.

Just to be a female was a stigma. My father openly showed me his resentment that I was born a daughter instead of a son and favored my brother in every way. As a result, I was the one who was beaten in his alcoholic rages. My mother, also female and subservient, was not in a position to stop him from this child abuse. In fact, she resented me as well. From her point of view, I was the cause of trouble in the family. If I hadn't been born a daughter, life with her husband would have been much easier.

With my family being so aggressively critical of me, naturally I was tempted to believe I was really wretched, deserving of hate, and unlikable. But I couldn't stop being myself. I had this inner determination that no matter how they treated me, I wouldn't give in. I wouldn't stop listening to my inner desires, and I actually began to pursue them. My refusal to accept and pursue the traditional oriental women's role brought the displeasure of peers and neighbors, of course, so that I really had nobody who believed in me.

Nobody, that is, except me - and the person who became my Master. At eight years of age, just when I should have been performing like a traditional oriental female, I was powerfully drawn to the martial art of Tae Kwon Do. I knew this was the only life I wanted, and my family, neighbors, everyone I encountered, applied enormous psychological and emotional pressure to stop me. My family even applied physical pressure, beating me and locking me in my room to keep me from practicing.

Your Silent Master Is Your Support

But I found a Ki Master who believed in me and was willing to teach me. He alone encouraged me to pursue the training, and to prevail against an entire culture. It would have been nice to have pats on the back from family and friends and friendly, supportive people while working toward my goals. It's nice for anyone. But the power of your real self - your Silent Master - is strong enough to love you and support you. Your Silent Master will bring to you, as it did to me, exactly what you need to fulfill yourself, whether it's one person, an army, or nobody. All you have to do is be yourself! Your *true* self. And your true self, as your awareness opens wider and wider, will show you - and bring you - everything you need.

Naturally this requires a decision on your part. I wasn't always a Grandmaster. I was a frightened little girl, and I had plenty of opportunities to make all kinds of excuses for not rising above my environment. But I made the personal decision not to accept the limitations of my surroundings, and you can do the same!

My fifth Silent Master Image says:

V

YOU HAVE THE POWER TO FULFILL YOUR DREAMS

> *Your Silent Master is completely*
> *aware, infinitely Intelligent, and*
> *ready to give you all the insight,*
> *information, and direction you need*
> *to fulfill your dreams, ambitions, and*
> *goals. In fact, this Consciousness is*
> *the Source of all your true desires.*

The force of my own real self, my own Silent Master, was a powerful factor in saving me from all the abuse, discrimination, and pressure, because it gave me particular desires which caused me to challenge these oppressors. It also gave me feelings of self-acceptance, determination, and perseverance to carry out my desires. It brought me my Master. It gave me direction on what decisions to make, what directions to take. And I *chose* to listen to this part of me rather than my external environment. To the best of my ability, I simply remained true to myself.

Of course it's very easy for me to say *be yourself*. It is not necessarily easy to *do*. In the next chapter, we will be looking more closely at this process of *being yourself*. For now, while we are talking about relationships, the point I'm making is that you must be willing to look at certain aspects of your personality as foreign to your true self, and be willing to go through the struggle to remove them. Otherwise, you're setting yourself up for relationship problems. And now, are you ready for one of the most powerful tools you possess to clear yourself of unwanted energy patterns? Here it is.

Forgiveness Dissolves Unwanted Energy Patterns

As you look back to your past and may discover areas where you did indeed accept negative or limiting beliefs about yourself, you will undoubtedly need to *forgive*; *release* anger, fear or guilt; and *let go*. Forgiveness does not mean you absolve anyone from wrongdoing. The wrong that was done is still wrong and will always be wrong. Rather, forgiveness helps you release the pattern so that it will not repeat in your life.

Some patterns are repeated even if we don't want them to be. For instance, people who were abused as children often become child abusers themselves. Since pain is almost always inevitable in life, we must learn from the things that hurt us. My childhood circumstances didn't overwhelm me because I took charge of my life and refused to be a victim.

It was wrong for my father to treat me as valueless, as bad and unworthy merely because I was a female. It was wrong for him to get drunk and beat me again and again. It was wrong to criticize me unjustly, humiliate me, and thwart my natural love and desires.

But what if I had made the decision to hate him instead of forgive him and go on with my pursuits? Hate has the effect of "solidifying" that which is hated, making it more real and enduring. Remember, we discussed in Chapter Two that all energy is the same energy, but colored differently by different beliefs. This means that hate is the same energy as love, but negatively colored, of course. Hate will energize and strengthen any situation just as love will, but it will energize and strengthen it negatively.

Hating my father, then, would have made his abusiveness more vivid, more enduring, more vibrant, in effect, and therefore more likely to manifest physically in my life not only from him but from others I would attract. My decision and determination to release myself from this oppressive environment was made possible by not hating.

Sometimes persons who come from a situation of child abuse - and who continue to hate the abusers without doing anything to dissolve the pattern - find themselves later in a spousal abuse situation. What's interesting about this is that even if the abused person ends the marriage as a solution, he or she ends up in another one just like it! This happens frequently, and we really see the power of energetic patterns at work here. Since the energetic pattern isn't being removed from the person's consciousness, merely leaving the marriage does not end the problem, and it repeats automatically.

As I mentioned before, this pattern can also produce a parent who abuses their own children. I even heard one of my students say desperately, "I don't want to treat my children the way I was treated, but I'm doing it anyway!" Again, we see that pattern isn't removed merely by knowing it's there, or by wishing and wanting it to go away.

It must be removed! Dissolved! And this is possible - with real forgiveness - if you have correctly identified the pattern and where you got it. If you go through therapy with a psychologist to work on this problem, ultimately the therapy must take you to this same place. You must get hold of that hurt place in yourself, feel the feelings, then consciously forgive in order to release it. And mean it! Then you can replace the old behavior with new patterns based on desirable energy. Do it now! Don't let anything stop you from exercising the freedom of forgiveness.

Become Aware of Repeating Patterns

One strong clue that some pattern from your past is operating is when the *same problem* appears in every relationship. For instance, one of my students, Molly, had a problem with jealous people in her life. Yes, she had many fine qualities that arouse admiration in some people and jealousy in others. But why was her circle of friends composed mainly of jealous friends who ended up trying to hurt her? She would start a new friendship only to have it end in some disappointing scenario where the friend would become resentful and openly attack her, compete in a destructive manner, or become threatened by her talent. *Why can't I have any good, supportive friends?* she would ask every time this happened.

Finally, after many days of examining this pattern and looking over past relationships, she had a startling realization...something she overlooked because it was so close to her and so much a part of her: her mother. Molly realized that all her friends were treating her exactly the way her mother treated her growing up. She reviewed scene after scene from her childhood and teen years, instances where her mother communicated jealousy, resentment, hostility over her looks, her talent, her intelligence, her boyfriends, her achievements, her activities, everything.

But she had grown so accustomed to her mother's subtle sarcasm, her cold and bitter attitude, that she never recognized it as a pattern of jealousy, and never rejected it. Instead, she accepted her mother's behavior as just "the way things are," and as a result, her mother's behavior became an energetic pattern of expectation for Molly. Unseen and unchallenged, a pattern like this operates invisibly, and goes on right under your nose until you identify it, consciously dissolve it with forgiveness, and replace it with the energy of new patterns.

Once Molly saw this pattern, she consciously formed new expectations about how people could regard her. In her patterns such as, My love brings love to others and love to me...My talents create joy for others and joy for me...I give the gifts I have received, and my gifts benefit everyone who receives them...Not everyone would find it necessary to use affirmations like this, but Molly had to work specifically in this area to completely change the type of relationships she was attracting. There is a similar exercise you can try at the end of this chapter. If you really want to hit a home run in the area of improving the quality of your relationships, make whatever effort it takes to perceive and clear away negative energy patterns!

Become Aware of Hidden Energy Patterns

There's another way relationships can show you undesirable patterns in your energy. Is there some quality you absolutely detest when it appears in other people? If so, look out! This may be the very quality which you possess but don't want to acknowledge because you detest it so much. This is not always the case, but very often it is.

For example, another of my students, Peter, thought of himself as a very calm, peaceful, and nonviolent person. And true enough, this is the way he acted, and he was quite clear about expressing his admiration for these qualities. So, why, then, did he constantly find himself in relationships with girlfriends who turned out to be "screamers," young women who voiced much anger and even expressed hostility physically. After this happened three times in a row, he realized it couldn't be just a coincidence. He had broken up with all three women and was now nervously trying to deal with a fourth turbulent relationship.

I'm not this way! he told me again and again. *I can't stand this behavior!* Yes, it was true Peter was "not this way." It was true he *acted* calm and quiet. But no, he was not free of anger. Peter was deeply afraid of anger, so afraid that he could not accept it in anyone, including himself. His way of avoiding anger was to create and rigidly enforce a calm exterior while ignoring all his anger inside.

As we've discussed in previous chapters, ignoring energy does not make it go away and does not change it. The anger in Peter was still *angry energy* whether or not he acknowledged it. Since this energy was in him, it resonated with others having the same energy. In effect, they were "acting out" his anger for him, showing it to him loud and clear.

So through relationships with others, Peter saw his own unacknowledged, unwanted, disowned energy. His angry energy, even though he didn't acknowledge it, literally resonated with and attracted angry people. The only way for Peter to dissolve this pattern was to learn not to be afraid of anger. He had to become willing to feel anger, learn how to express it constructively, and learn how to *let it go*. When we discussed your emotional body in Chapter Two, we saw that emotions must *flow* to be healthy, never denied, never dammed up in any way for any reason. Anger correctly expressed is anger dissolved.

Serving Versus Controlling

So far, we've been discussing how to improve the quality of relationships by identifying and removing undesirable energy patterns from yourself. We've discussed how this process prevents these undesirable patterns from manifesting in relationships.

Now I'd like to move on to another major way to improve all your relationships. This involves an attitude, or a super-attitude, we could say, because it really boils down to a whole *approach* to life: serving.

Unfortunately, the concept of serving has developed some bad publicity. We may think of serving as a menial, thankless, or powerless activity. But quite the contrary, true serving is a powerful and pervasive form of love that benefits the server as much as the served (if not more). It's sometimes true that the world does not appreciate the service and generosity of true servers. But it doesn't matter, because the servers know the gains, rewards, and true freedom that come with acting from this point of power.

Why is serving an expression of power and freedom? The answer revolves around "giving." Serving is the attitude of giving rather than taking, giving rather than controlling. Giving people are powerful because they *have* something to give and they *know* what they have. Knowing what you have, especially if you know the Source of what you have, means that you can manifest infinitely. What freedom this is!

My sixth Silent Master Image in my book, <u>Seven Steps to Inner Power</u>, says:

VI
YOU ARE COMPLETE, PEACEFUL, AND FULFILLED

> *Your Silent Master expresses*
> *completeness, fulfillment, harmony,*
> *peace, joy, and love, and imparts*
> *these qualities to everything It*
> *creates.*

This image reminds us that through our connection with the life force of the universe, we are complete. We possess the *potential* to express or manifest anything and everything that is part of the universe. Any object, any concept, any feeling, any quality, any condition, circumstance or event. Being complete does not mean we have nothing more to learn, do, be, or become. Being complete means we have the potential to accomplish anything that is naturally a part of the universe.

There is a Biblical passage where Jesus said, "For everyone who *has* will be given more, and he will have an abundance. Whoever *does not have*, even what he has will be taken from him" (Matthew 25:29). This is a way of describing the law of "like attracts like." Clearly, if you *have* a realization of your Silent Master Consciousness, you have a connection to the source of all, and no wonder you can manifest abundance! The consciousness of abundance creates abundance.

If, on the other hand, you *do not have* an awareness of the power and potential of your Silent Master, if you do not have a consciousness of abundance, you cannot manifest abundance. A consciousness of lack creates lack. People who know they have an abundance can be free and easy givers. People who feel a constant sense of lack become takers, even manipulators and controllers. Do you want more abundance in your life? Then become more generous! Create abundance in your own way first, and then you'll see it come back to you.

Fear Creates Lack

We were just discussing how patterns formed in vulnerable childhood years often go on to manifest in many different ways. Again, we can look to the past to see how a consciousness of lack develops, which then leads to a controlling state of mind.

When you are an infant and small child, you are totally dependent on others for your survival. You must get what you need, or you will die, and you feel this clearly. If you were in a situation where your needs were not met sufficiently or consistently, you developed a fear of abandonment. And that fear pattern may still be within you now.

This pattern puts people in a weak position, feeling a constant inability to get or have all that they need. As a result, they also feel the need to manipulate or control others to *make sure* they get what they need. It's a distrusting posture, based on their previous experience of not being able to trust those who were supposed to care for them. Although they may get what they want sometimes, it is a condition of lack, and these people often experience loss. Just as Jesus indicated, their sense of lack causes even what they have to be taken from them.

This is exactly the opposite state of mind from serving. People who serve do so because they know that their giving not only enriches others, but themselves as well. Serving creates abundance for the giver (which means they have *even more* to give). In the spirit of like attracts like, their giving *creates* giving, including giving to themselves! When they find themselves receiving, it's their own *giving* being given to them.

Giving returns to you in other ways besides physical or material ways. When I was serving my Master, for instance, it seemed that I was giving and doing everything for him. Later I realized I had been nourishing my spiritual being in the process. The giving demanded that I release a lot of self-centered physical, emotional, and mental desires and develop spiritual qualities such as greater love, gratitude, peace, and humility.

How rich your relationships can be when you and the other person approach each other with the intent to serve. You serve not by giving up who you are to cater to someone else's needs. Rather, you serve by *expressing* who you are, giving your gifts to the other person in the process. When both parties do this, you are both being true to yourselves, and you are both bringing the best you have to offer to the relationship.

Serving Is Unconditional Love

What more can there be to love than being true to yourself and giving your truth everywhere to everyone? This is serving. When you love this way, there are no "conditions" placed on your expression of love. You simply remain true to yourself with everyone, and give your best to them. If your truth is not acceptable to someone, then at that moment in time and space, you simply cannot be together with that person.

When you love unconditionally in serving this way, your relationship cannot be based on need or fear. Recently, one of my students, Bob, was confiding in me about the "divorce talk" that was going on between him and his wife. We had spoken about this before, and there were some good indications that Bob and Janine's lives were going in very different directions and that a divorce might be appropriate.

At first it seemed like Bob was depressed and sad about having his love rejected by Janine. But looking closer, the actual state he was in was *fear*. Bob was terrified. He described how he wasn't able to sleep or eat and told me of his desperate attempts to make more money so maybe she would stay. He was not looking to see where he or she might be thwarting each other's growth by making selfish or inappropriate demands on each other. He was not looking for new avenues of learning and growth.

Instead, as we talked more, it became clear that the main reason he did not want the divorce was because "there was nothing better" to be offered, and as he said, "he didn't want to be alone."

This is far from a state of unconditional love. I never heard Bob say in all his anguish, "I love her." I heard him say, "I need her." This relationship was based more on need - a desire to take or receive - than on love, a desire to serve. Janine was needing Bob to fulfill her material wishes, and Bob was needing Janine to keep him from being alone. In this situation, nothing was being given to the relationship. They were draining each other emotionally, mentally, and physically. And this kind of relationship is bound to fail, bound to dry up from lack of nourishment.

Expressing unconditional love, one says about a marriage relationship, *I want to be with you because I choose to be...Giving my love to you brings me even more joy than I have alone...* But Bob was saying, *I want to be with you because I need to be...Without your presence I feel alone.* A marriage based on this attitude may have some affection in it, even some sharing or other good qualities, but it does not have the power and potential for growth, development, and expansion that unconditional love brings to a marriage.

Of course, it takes strength, generosity, and an awareness of your inner power and freedom to love unconditionally. It takes knowing who you are, knowing your Silent Master Consciousness, knowing how much you have to give, and that you can live alone with your richness as easily as with someone else. Marriage is a choice in this situation, not a necessity.

If all of this seems out of reach, too idealistic to be practical, all you have to do is pursue the goal of expressing unconditional love. Just start! If it's true that you want a good and happy relationship with someone, then you must have a good and happy relationship with yourself first. There's no other way! When you reach the point where you are happy and fulfilled being alone, where you are aware of the richness, fullness, peace, and power of your Silent Master, you are in the best position to attract the right someone to *share* this happiness successfully and harmoniously. And when you're ready to share your life, you will have more success if you understand something about balance - which we will look at now.

The Balance of Yin and Yang

In this chapter, we've talked about two ways of enhancing your relationships: first, by eliminating negative energy patterns so that they don't manifest in your relationships; and second, by approaching other people with the attitude of serving.

Now here's a third way to help bring harmony to your relationships: honoring the balance of yin and yang embodied in both partners.

As we discussed previously, yin and yang represent the two forces constantly changing in the energetic motion of the universal life force. You may recall in Chapter One that I described yin and yang, two opposite energetic states.

Male and female are two opposite energetic states, male corresponding to the yang energy, female corresponding to the yin energy. Neither is superior or inferior to the other. They are equal and opposite, and have their unique characteristics. Both are necessary to create unity because they help define each other. We could say male means not-female and female means not-male. Please understand that when I talk about female and male as being yin and yang, I am not talking about sexuality or sexual preference. Rather, I'm talking about the mental or spiritual *qualities* which can be described as male or female, qualities which belong to men and women alike.

Throughout many cultures and much of history, yang qualities have traditionally been assigned to men and yin qualities have been embodied somewhat exclusively by the women. For instance, let's take the yin-yang qualities of *passive-active*. As we look around the globe, we can see that males have (in recent times, at least) traditionally taken the active-yang role as the aggressive leaders in politics, the workplace, and in most homes. Females have traditionally taken a more passive-yin role, being the followers, nurturers, caretakers, and supporters of the males.

Fortunately, this very restricted view is changing. Many people are now realizing that yin and yang qualities belong to men and women *alike* and that *both* sexes should be free to express *both* yin and yang qualities. There are appropriate times for men and women to express their yin and yang qualities. If a woman is a business executive, she may express her male-yang quality of active aggression in the corporate workplace or when playing racquetball. A man may have to bring out his female-yin quality of passive receptivity when troubleshooting his computer problem or attending an art class.

Simple Respect Is Love

Why should men or women have to play a restricted role devoid of a balance of yin and yang qualities? We need to honor *both* qualities in our partners and give them the space to express their completeness.

This idea of honoring both yin and yang qualities in others boils down to simple *respect*. When a man or woman has spent the entire day actively at work, the evening may be the time for their passive state of rest and recuperation. We need to honor this energetic change by allowing it to happen without obstruction. When a man or woman has spent most of their life developing yang qualities necessary for competition in the commercial world, they may need a period of time devoted to yin qualities such as meditation, introspection, or quiet creativity.

We need to be sensitive to these energetic changes in our partners, because the change between yin and yang is the very essence of our life force. Since our life force constantly changes between these two energetic states, we need to respect the beauty and necessity of both.

Respect is a powerfully beautiful way to express love. Generally, we use the word love rather carelessly. We say we love apple pie, love our car, love to go shopping...Perhaps expressions like these tend to disconnect us from deeper feelings of true love that includes respect.

Instead of saying, *I love you* to someone, what could you say to mean the same thing? I *trust* you...I *believe* in you...I *know* you...I *value* you...If you think of all the words you can to replace the word love, I think you'll find respect at or near the top of your list. I *respect you* is very definitely a far-reaching expression of love.

Respect means that you are in a place of unconditional love that we talked about earlier. You are accepting another person without any conditions being placed on your truth or your honesty. You allow them to be who they are, and you remain true to yourself. If you are incompatible, if you cannot accept their values, then you must part. But you part with respect.

Respect does not mean that you condone someone or something that you consider wrong, untrue, or incompatible with your real values. In fact, you may have to take some action to correct a distorted situation such as when you see someone stealing. Rather, respect simply means you acknowledge that the wrong is a situation that can change - like everything else in this world that is in constant change - and that you give it the space and opportunity to change, perhaps by your taking some appropriate action.

Respect involves a certain humility, knowing what you are called to change and what you aren't called to change. When you are really in touch with your Silent Master, you are sensitive to every situation you're in, and you feel guided into appropriate action or non-action. Sometimes the greatest teachers feel guided to let their students take a wrong path as the best way to teach them. Sometimes, the same teacher will yank a student back on the road forcefully.

It is the same for us when we're in relationships, either as spouses or parents or friends. There are no hard and fast rules as to the best way to respect others' individuality and integrity. The only rule is to reach for your Silent Master Consciousness with the best listening ear you can. Our Silent Master, that connection we have with infinite intelligence, knows the best path for all of us to take. It knows how and where each of us intersects with others. It can help you understand why certain people are in your life, what you can learn from each other, and when or if it's time to move on.

As I mentioned earlier, your own Silent Master is your first and original relationship. It is the infinite, eternal part of you that loves you and all the universe unconditionally because it is Love! Love is your true, pure, original energy. This Love is within you now, and it will create and attract beautiful, growing relationships in every area of your life. Your task is to do everything you can to open up to it, let it in, and express it!

Exercises

1. Here's an exercise to help you identify negative energy patterns that may be operating in your life.

Step One: Start by taking a look at some discordant situation right now, and look to the past to see where it's happened before (it almost always *has*). Put the pattern into a sentence or two, i.e., "I attract situations of betrayal," "Most of my relationships are with dishonest people who cheat me," "My poor attendance gets me fired from every job," "I can't be on time anywhere I go"...whatever...

Step Two: Once the pattern is identified, identify the mental and emotional energy involved. Completing this simple sentence should do the trick - if you're honest using above examples:

> *I attract situations of betrayal* because I believe
> that _____, and this makes me feel _____.
> *Or, my poor attendance gets me fired from every job*
> because I believe that _____, and this makes
> me feel _____.

Realize that these are energy distortions, not the true state of your real self. Look again to the past to see where you first thought this way. When did you first feel this way? Were you attacked and made to feel hurt, unappreciated, and unvalued? Look closely at your first relationships and your childhood. You may see where it started and how the pattern went on to repeat over and over.

Step Three: Create affirmations that describe your real self, your true energy, even though you aren't manifesting this behavior. If you said, for instance, "*I attract situations of betrayal because I believe that people will want to attack me, and this makes me feel hurt, unappreciated, and unvalued,*" perhaps your affirmations might be: "*I am pure love and loving. Others feel my love and their love arises and returns to me and everyone. My beauty, my gifts, my love, my talents bring joy to me and joy to others. I give my gifts to everyone, and their gifts are shared with me. We are all one in an ocean of love where our light moves to and fro from one to another, giving and receiving with joy, trust and love..."*

Step Four: Now enter formal meditation, and when you have slowed your breathing and the flow of thoughts, let your affirmations move like waves across the space of your mind, creating the picture you desire to see.

2. After some practice with these four steps, take a close look at some specific relationship in your life, one where you are having difficulty. Identify the nature of the problem very specifically and clearly. Look to see if you've had the same problem before or if it's being repeated right now in other current relationships. Then, similar to the previous exercise, search through your past or your upbringing to see if this is where the pattern first developed. Now you're in a position to replace the pattern with a better one.

Meditation

With the purity, clarity, and love
of my Silent Master awareness,
I have the insight to perceive all energy
patterns operating in my life.
With my purity,
I perceive undesirable patterns
obstructing the energy of my true self...
With my clarity,
I replace obstructive patterns with true ones
to bring harmony, peace, and trust to my relationships...
With my love,
I forgive myself and others
for all mistakes and wrongdoing,
understanding that we are all made
of the same pure, original ki...
realizing there is only love
in our Silent Master Consciousness...
knowing that each of us
desires, deserves, and can attain
the freedom of expressing forgiveness.

CHAPTER FIVE

Ki and Your Health

Without you,
I am nowhere.
With you,
I am now here
This moment, and forever.
You are everything I am,
Or could be,
Or will be,
As we dance our dance together
Creating forms as yet undreamed.

Health Is Wholeness

I wasn't surprised when I learned that the English words *health* and *heal* developed from an original root word meaning whole. Why? From an energy point of view, you experience health when your physical, emotional, mental, and spiritual bodies are working as one unit, as a whole unit, without distortions or blockages in the flow of your energy from one body to another.

Long before the synthetic drugs and modern surgery techniques of today's medicine, healers in ancient traditions worked directly with the *energies* of a sick patient. These traditions recognized that when the physical body was ill, there were other energies out of order besides the physical. So the healers used remedies which altered the patient's *entire* energy field to restore healthy balance. Acupuncture (or acupressure) was used to dissolve blockages where ki energy was not flowing or circulating freely; the laying on of hands was used to transfer and balance energy; mantras, chanting, or prayers combined with drumming or other musical instruments were vibrational tools used to impact the patient's energy field with sound; and natural herbs were a way of grounding the patient with healthy earth energy, the first material medicine. Some modern drugs are still derived from herbs, but today we produce many chemically synthesized medicines.

Even though these treatments are not widespread today, disease is still an energy disorder just as it was then.

Disease is just that - *dis-ease*, a lack of ease - in your energy field. I am not at all criticizing modern medicine. But I am saying that we can assist or enhance our modern healing techniques by embracing an even larger picture regarding ill health. For the most part, modern medicine treats only the physical body, as though that is the only part of you that is ill. When we understand that disease is an energetic disorder that impacts our mental, emotional, and spiritual bodies as well, we are in a much better position to restore health - or *wholeness*.

If you are working with a physical problem, maybe now is the time to give this approach a try! Look closely with me in this chapter at how the energy in your four bodies can work together producing health or disease.

Disease Can Be an Energy Disorder

Let's begin by looking at a very good example of how distorted energy in the emotional, mental, and spiritual bodies can produce a physical picture of total ill health, a diseased condition that doctors failed to correct with physical treatment alone.

A young couple, Ray and Pauline, and their young son Joshua, four-years-old, were training at my school. I was aware that Joshua was particularly frail, and I noticed that his attendance was constantly interrupted by one health problem after another. First it was an ear infection, then strep throat, then a bronchial infection, on and on.

Finally, after an especially long absence, Pauline called to say that Joshua was in the hospital. Apparently this current problem had started with a flu, but this time, he wasn't recovering. He had already lost five pounds partly because he had no appetite. His bowels and bladder were not functioning consistently, and his body was limp and lifeless.

Worst of all, the antibiotics and other treatments the doctors ordered were having no effect whatsoever. Of course they ran all kinds of tests, but nothing definitive came to light, and Joshua's condition simply worsened day by day.

Immunity Is Self Versus Not-Self

It was obvious to me that Joshua's immune system wasn't functioning properly, even though the tests for leukemia and cancer had turned up negative. Your immune system is your body machinery which eliminates infections and toxins. It works by distinguishing between self and not-self. When your immune system spots something not-self in your system - like an alien microbe - it attacks the microbe in any number of ways to eliminate it. Your healthy immune system knows very clearly what is or isn't a natural element in your healthy "self." Joshua's immune system was not doing this job effectively. Instead of attacking and eliminating the germs behind all his infections, or the toxins contributing to his present condition, his immune system (as well as his bladder and bowels) seemed tired, overwhelmed, or just burned out.

When Pauline finally approached me with the problem, I had the opportunity to begin dealing with the energetic problem. Why did it appear as if Joshua - that is, Joshua's physical self - having difficulty distinguishing between self and not-self?

As we discussed in the last chapter, children are very vulnerable to the energy of their immediate family or the people responsible for taking care of them. Children do not have a strongly developed self-concept, and therefore have little or no defenses to protect themselves from hostile and aggressive energy. That's why, for the most part, they rely on parents to defend and protect them in every way physically, emotionally, mentally, and spiritually.

I was aware that Ray and Pauline lived in a state of nearly constant conflict. This warfare created an atmosphere of tension, anger, and hostility which was not only out in the open, but stirring and broiling in their times of silence and withdrawal as well. In short, there was no escape for Joshua in this household, no shelter, no safe, peaceful haven anywhere.

Children like Joshua are simply not equipped to defend their energy field in this kind of atmosphere. If you've spent time with children, you may have noticed that in stressful situations which most adults can manage without upset, children will very likely develop stomach aches.

Without adult psychological defenses to block out negative energy, they absorb it, and have no idea why or how. *I don't feel good*, they'll say. In a matter of minutes or hours, however, after the stressful situation is cleared away, they're happy, normal, and "well" again.

So Joshua could not feel his *self* in his home - his true self. Instead, he was subjected to a constant barrage of alien, "not-self" energy, negative energy, that was literally overwhelming. He had no "immunity" to it because, as a child, he hadn't had the life experience to build psychological defenses. He could not process this energy, and he could not get away from it because he was dependent on these two people. So the negativity simply solidified in his physical body, producing a picture of a completely malfunctioning, lifeless, weak, and disintegrating physical "self" unable to defend itself against the "not-self" elements.

Changing Energy Can Bring Healing

In a nutshell, the parents' constant warfare was a factor in Joshua's dis-ease. Their hostile, aggressive negativity was overwhelming Joshua's energy. Of course, I couldn't say this to Ray and Pauline directly as I'm saying it to you. They loved Joshua very dearly and deeply and would have been so horrified at the idea they were hurting their son, that they probably would have denied it. So I began an indirect approach, at first, to help restore Joshua to his rightful health.

One evening I took a group of my instructors to the hospital. With Ray and Pauline's permission, we formed a circle around Joshua, and I began to channel energy to his body, working as I have been trained by my Master to balance and revitalize his energy. Almost immediately he began to respond. The color returned to his face, his breathing was deeper, and he became more vibrant.

Joshua continued to improve enough to be discharged. But the environment at home had not changed. In a very short time, Joshua was falling back into the old condition, losing his appetite, losing weight, losing strength, losing immunity to simple colds and infections. But fortunately, by this time, Ray and Pauline were ready to begin working on their own energy. I began counseling with them on a regular basis to change the conditions of their relationship and home life.

Within only six months, there was a dramatic improvement. Joshua no longer had the dark circles under his eyes or the unhealthy green tint to his skin. He was more radiant, active, stronger, heavier and more alive than ever before in his life! The energy of his parents, environment and body had changed, and we saw the visible results in his new healthy body.

Are you perhaps thinking, *Well, it's fine to heal an energy problem like Joshua's with energy...but I have a physical problem! I need physical treatment.* Don't forget, if you're saying this, that Joshua did have a physical problem. The physical manifestation just didn't happen to have one of the traditional medical names.

If you have a physical problem that *does* have a traditional medical name, you may also have an energy problem just as Joshua did. Dis-eased energy may manifest in the physical body as disease. Medical science has given many of these conditions specific names. But regardless of the name, or lack of a name, distorted energy may still be the cause and substance of disease. Of course there's nothing wrong with having physical medical treatment. But the treatment may not be completely effective if you don't also deal with the energy of your other bodies. I have students who have used energy training to heal a variety of traditional medical problems, including psoriasis, thyroid conditions, skin rashes, bleeding ulcers, epilepsy, arthritis, asthma, chronic acne, and cancer, to name a few.

Strengthen Your Immune System

I shared Joshua's story with you is because it really illustrates the importance of the immune system, that which distinguishes between self and not-self. If you think about it, nearly every disease you can think of involves some kind of "alien" element which the body must destroy or eliminate. So healing any disease you may have ultimately boils down to getting your immune system to really kick in and kick out the offenders. And this means getting a clear concept of your true self, your true energy.

It is possible that within you right now there might be cells which *could* become cancerous, but your immune system is using one of its many resources to prevent that from happening. Your ability - reflected in your body's immune system - to distinguish between true natural self and false sick self is key to maintaining health!

How important it is, then, for you to be aware of the energy of your *true self* in all your bodies. Your physical immune system, like every other aspect of your physical being, functions according to the state of your emotional, mental, and spiritual bodies. When you are true to your real, original self - and consciously strive to keep your energy pure - your immune system reflects this, and operates effectively in eliminating "invasions" from outside sources (outside thoughts, outside emotions, outside toxins). If you distort your true, original energy by holding negative concepts, feelings, emotions, and toxins, your immune system will reflect this distortion in being unable to eliminate diseased conditions.

There are already statistics, for instance, which show that cancer is most likely to develop in patients who have undergone a period of deep depression, perhaps for the previous two years. The patient may have lost a spouse through death or divorce and has been grieving for the past two years. Of course, there are many other contributing causes for cancer, but let's just look at how depression deadens your immune system such that an effective fight becomes impossible.

Grieving is a normal, natural, healthy flow of emotion. It should be done at the time of the sad event and then let go. But depression is a distorted energy state. It is a condition of *holding* grief, damming it up in the person's emotional body, where it should normally be allowed to *flow* and *dissolve*. Reflecting the state of the emotional body, the physical immune system likewise dams up and *stops operating* properly.

All four bodies work together. In a condition of depression the mental body is saying "I am *stuck* in this condition of grief, with no solutions, no alternatives to my aloneness and isolation." The emotional body is saying "I *feel* incredible pain being forced to endure this situation where there is no relief in sight." The spiritual body is saying, "I may as well *shut down* or die since there is no way out, no hope, nothing I can feel optimistic about that would warrant continuing to move life force through this body." So no wonder the physical body reflects this distress with a disabled immune system! One that won't fight! The physical immune system reflects the depressed state of the other bodies, grinds to a halt, and shuts down. In this state, you don't have the defense you need if there is some disruption in your body like microbes or cancer cells.

A healthy energy system constantly eliminates cancer cells and any and all toxins or alien elements which cause disease. That's why the carcinogens in our food and environment affect some people but certainly not all people. A depressed person has a depressed immune system and may not survive an enemy invasion like a healthy person could.

Healing Involves All Your Bodies

So far, I've been trying to make it clear that all your bodies are impacted by what goes on in each one of them. We've discussed in previous chapters how your physical body displays the visible picture of this collective activity. We see our physical body, of course; but since we don't "see" our emotional, mental, and spiritual bodies in the same way, we are inclined to treat all our physical symptoms without working with our other energies in our other bodies.

An overweight person, for instance, typically thinks that a physical diet will change the physical body. And it will - maybe - but until the emotional energy is discharged, the physical body will not remain changed. Here are some other situations which appear to be physical problems, but which have their roots in other bodies. Do you find yourself saying something like:

Since I moved to my new house, I've had insomnia.

Since I met Sally, I've had terrible bladder problems.

Since my wife got pregnant, I've started having migraines.

Since my mother-in-law moved in, I've had this rash.

Since my business has been doing well, I've developed an ulcer.

Since many common health problems have their roots in your "unseen bodies," let's look at them more closely to see where and how you can experience better energy. This is something you deserve. Your birthright is health and wholeness, so let's work together to achieve this!

A Sense of Separation Creates Disease

As we've been discussing, you experience a state of health - or wholeness - when your ki energy is flowing freely through all your bodies without obstructions or blocks. What is a block? It is something that prevents the normal, healthy manifestation of your ki energy. A block is an emotion, thought, belief, concept, or pattern which is manifesting as an undesirable picture in your physical body. Very often you aren't aware of blocks in your energy until you see this physical problem and desire to heal it. In a moment, we will look more closely at handling a common block we all experience - anger - and a sample manifestation of it, such as a growth on your hand.

What causes blocks? Essentially, you are likely to develop blocks in your energy when you have a sense of separation. There are three main ways you experience separation:

1. feeling separate from your Silent Master Consciousness, from its purity, power, and originality;
2. feeling a sense of separation between your bodies, commonly called the body-mind split;
3. feeling separate from your environment and others.

Of course, anger is a complex subject, and there are many related causes for it. But let's look at how these three types of separation help create anger, a powerful energy block which can produce a wide range of physical symptoms. As we focus on anger, bear in mind that most everything we're saying about the creation of anger applies to creation of other not-self states such as greed, jealousy, hatred, resentment, etc.

But first, let's look at your *un-separated* true state. What are you like when you're consciously at one with your Silent Master? Then we can look at what arises that distorts this energy, producing unhealthy physical states.

In a healthy state, where you are aware of your Silent Master Consciousness, you experience all external conditions passing through your experience as constantly changing events that have no permanence. Since you know the impermanence of all events, joy-producing events have no more enduring significance than sorrow-producing events. They are merely changing scenes flowing through your unchanging Silent Master.

So instead, you experience a pattern of harmony underneath this constantly changing picture, and you feel a quiet joy *unaffected* by fluctuating circumstances. This state is a kind of detachment, but not a dry, unfeeling detachment because you also feel a calm, blissful peace and joy.

This unending, unchangeable bliss and joy of your Silent Master Consciousness has been described in many traditions. In its highest "frequencies," it is an all-encompassing bliss, an ecstatic bliss that is so indescribable it cannot be compared to ordinary emotions. In its lower frequencies, it is felt as emotion, as an inner smiling joy that is so peaceful, you can truly be detached from all circumstances, letting everything around you change and flow.

To maintain this detachment, you need to identify with it. You need to know, consciously know, "This is me." What happens to interrupt this blissful state? We begin to react to circumstances outside us, and this makes us lose our detachment. We begin attaching to the material picture and we literally "forget" who we are as our Silent Master Consciousness. This is where the sense of separation begins. Look now to see how something like the following may have happened to you.

Separation Is a Cause of Fear and Powerlessness

Some kind of stress in the world out there occurs, and we are tempted out of our peaceful, stable Silent Master state. We begin to react with some measure of *fear: What is the right thing to do? What if I don't make the right decision? How will I find the strength to go on? How will I overcome this? What if I get hurt? What's going to happen to me?* Notice that this fear is coming from a sense of separation from your Silent Master. Poised as your Silent Master Consciousness, you have a peaceful sense of "knowing" in all situations, and you are automatically guided fearlessly into right action, right thought, right everything. But now, feeling separated from this poise, feeling yourself right in the middle of stress, you have this sense of fear - to whatever degree.

Fear is a feeling of powerlessness. If you don't find the strength to return to your Silent Master Consciousness for power, you will attempt to regain power in a lesser way. And now we can see how anger arises out of a separation from your Silent Master. Anger is a way of expressing power when you feel you don't have any. Or put it this way: Anger is an attempt to feel powerful when you aren't. And true enough, it may even lead you into some physical expression of power, usually negative, of course, like striking something or someone. Anger almost always produces a verbal assault, if not a physical one. (By the way, consider how other negative energy blocks - hatred, greed, jealousy, etc. - are also attempts to feel and regain power.)

Anger also gives you a sense of power in the sense of "hardening" your field (sometimes this is reflected in your physical body as hard lump or tumor). Hardening your field with anger is an attempt to keep hostile, aggressive, or alien energy from penetrating your field. How? Anger gives you a strong sensation of radiating energy outward, and you feel that if your energy is going out, nothing can get in. True enough, in an angry state, you are radiating energy outward, but it is negative energy and produces negative effects! If, for example, you have been living in an abusive environment, you may be going around in a chronically angry state to "defend" yourself. Your anger may indeed keep some hostile elements at bay, but your "holding" *will* solidify in some kind of unpleasant physical condition. Since it is a not-self state, anger is an energy distortion - a dis-eased condition - and will manifest as such if not discharged.

Separation Is a Cause of Conflict

Let's say your anger is directed at a person. Again, we have separation. You feel separated from this person. If you were aware of your Silent Master Consciousness, the place where all individuals connect in unity, you would feel your oneness with this person (and all persons), and you wouldn't be inclined to assault your own connection.

The reason why we see so much inhumanity to humankind carried out with anger, greed, or jealousy is because we feel keenly separated by our skin boundaries, and we have forgotten that we are one with each other in our Silent Master Consciousness. In most cases, we would never treat our "self" the way we treat other people. Yet, in effect, we are hurting our self when we hurt others because *we are connected.* All of your body parts are connected, aren't they? When one part of your body is "hurting" you, do you retaliate by angrily hurting it in return? No. You take an appropriate healing action. Why not treat our fellow humans the same?

We *are* truly members of *one* family of consciousness, sharing *one* energy. When we rise to the consciousness of our oneness, it's possible to *feel* what our "brother" feels. At that time there's no question of our connection to each other because it can be felt. Unfortunately, right now, until we reach this point in consciousness, we must simply accept that we are connected and act accordingly.

Separation Is a Cause of Energy Blocks

Plus, there's another kind of separation going on with anger. Some of us were never allowed to feel our anger honestly and openly as we grew up, nor allowed to safely discharge it. Some of us were taught that anger is bad and may have been punished in some way for expressing it. As a result of holding anger, damming it up in your emotional body, a physical problem may have developed, a metabolism problem, for instance, like hypoglycemia. Feeling that consciousness - which can be experienced as holding anger - is separate from the body, it if difficult to connect the anger with the physical hypoglycemia.

This is the body/mind split, where you don't recognize that body and mind are one - different aspects of your ki energy working together. In this situation, you don't see that the blood sugar problem and its accompanying mood swings can be related to the anger in your emotional body, so you don't heal your emotional body, and your physical problem can simply go on and on.

Now we're ready to look at a solution to this problem. You have the ability to influence and maintain health. Are you ready now to take responsibility for the quality of your energy? Here's how you can do it.

Transform Your Diseased Energy States

Regaining your connection with your Silent Master Consciousness is the ultimate healing solution for many problems. It bestows the peaceful, joyous, and loving high frequency energy that harmonizes and stabilizes all other energies in your being. If it seems really hard to regain your Silent Master Consciousness when you are so "pulled out" into the whirl of mental, emotional, and physical stress, there's one thing that can help you.

Remember this: *All* energy, all negative energy, all positive energy, is made of the one, pure original ki energy which is your Silent Master. Instead of regarding your stress as distress, regard it as your Silent Master energy in disguise!

That is the truth! All distortions of energy, such as fear, greed, jealousy, and anger, are capable of being transformed back into their original state.

The first step to take in transforming these negative expressions of energy is to *accept and acknowledge* them. This means don't try to "cut yourself off" from them, ignore them, or try to convince yourself you don't feel them. Your anger, even though it is a distortion, is ultimately your Silent Master ki energy. You want to *keep* your energy - and transform it, not throw it away.

Secondly, explore the energy distortion. Whatever it is, it is telling you something about a condition, person, or event in your life that wants your attention! As we discussed in Chapter Two, when we talked about "emotional bubbles" like jealousy, loaded with information, there's a reason for every feeling you feel, and something to learn. Believe me, when you listen to why you're angry, what beliefs you're accepting about yourself in order to feel angry, you will get an earful!

Thirdly, discharge your energy distortions by feeling them. There are a couple of therapists who actually have a technique of telling patients to make their energy distortions bigger. These therapists have found that temporarily exaggerating the distortion - feeling it even more intensely and dramatically than normal - has the effect of making you see it more clearly and discharge it more easily and rapidly. It's not surprising that this technique works well in dissolving negative energy patterns, since we've seen how the opposite policy of "holding" and "damming up" has such destructive effects. One way to release anger is to express your anger to someone you trust. Let that person see and hear how angry you are. This alone can do wonders in discharging that energy.

And fourthly, take some action to replace the distorted energy pattern with another way of thinking, feeling, acting. It's fine and well to say, "Yes, I see how my chronic anger is an attempt to defend myself against hostile negative energy in my history..." Good, so what are you going to do now? What changes are you going to make in your environment, your attitudes, or your way of reacting to events around you? What are you going to do in the way of meditation or visualization to create and attract different energy patterns in your life?

Positive Energy Transforms Negative Energy

What do you do about a problem when you don't know the cause? What if, for instance, you find a growth on your hand and you don't know why it's there? Fortunately, since your bodies are all connected, when you place your mind on a problem, in your physical body for example, this automatically stimulates an awareness of its impact in your other bodies. You can access this information to help you heal yourself. That is, if your physical problem has an emotional distortion behind it, contacting the physical problem will stimulate the emotional connection. You will feel the emotional connection in some way, and by using this information, you can make changes which can affect the physical picture.

If you have a growth on your hand you're at least aware that the growth is not part of your natural self. So you ask *why is it manifesting...could this be a representation of a not-self element?* But it could be you have no idea. Now what do you do?

The first thing to do is consciously *be aware* that your true self, your true ki energy, could be right where the growth is. Although it's taking form in a negative picture, by changing your energy you can influence this manifestation to change into a picture of your normal ki energy. In a quiet state of meditation, such as the inner eyes meditation described previously, you visualize your body perfectly whole, healthy, and free of the distortion. In this case, you see your hand clearly in your visualization in its normal, healthy condition.

Notice that we are not attacking the problem, not doing anything to the growth. That would energize it. Nor are we ignoring it. That would leave it intact. Instead we are realizing - making real - your true self in the form of a visualization. This has a wonderful and powerful effect. Before long, maybe soon, maybe later, this visualization of wholeness, purity, and health "forces out" the offending thought, emotion, concept, or pattern. When you fill your consciousness with the energy of perfection, the distortion necessarily becomes more clear and easy to see.

Sometimes it can happen that you will consciously realize, in a moment of insight or inspiration, exactly what's behind the negative picture and change your consciousness right on the spot to influence healing. For instance, one day as you're doing your visualization of your healthy hand, you may suddenly remember an ancient hatred you have for someone. You had forgotten all about it, and as you feel all the old emotion arising - seemingly "out of the blue"- you become aware of how you never let go of all the pain, anger, and hate from this scenario. That's why you can still feel it. But if you take steps then and there to deeply forgive the persons and let it go, your body will be freer to fight the growth. Don't be surprised if sometime later you find that your healing has accelerated and that you are feeling much better.

It also can happen that you never really find out what was behind your physical problem. The visualization of health and wholeness sometimes removes the offending cause and picture without your awareness of it, and one day you realize it's "just gone." Filling your consciousness with images of perfection and purity doesn't leave room for negative patterns to exist and manifest.

Here again, as we've been discussing throughout this chapter, the emphasis is on maintaining a conscious awareness of your *unity* with the harmony, beauty, peace, and perfection of your true ki, your Silent Master. When a negative condition has manifested, we don't want to "dance" with it, so to speak. Instead, we want to dance with our pure, original Silent Master Consciousness and allow its force to transform our negative picture into one of wholeness and perfection.

Gain Strength: Learn from Your Pain

Pain, distress, and physical illness are manifestations of our own energy. That's why they are an inevitable part of life. Instead of being defeated, crushed, or disillusioned about these things, allow them to at least teach you something. Why endure pain for nothing? Since you're going to encounter it, and since it's your own energy, make it serve you!

If you refuse to feel your mental and emotional pain, it will go on to take form physically in some way. By physically, I don't necessarily mean a body illness only. Refusing to deal with mental and emotional pain - simply because it's painful - leads quite directly to a false self concept and behavior patterns of addiction, which only compound the pain.

As I pointed out in Chapter Two, in order to cut off one emotion, such as painful grief or sorrow, it's necessary to cut off all emotion. That's the way the system works. A person who does this will have no valid emotions, and will need to seek other sources of "feeling." He or she shuts out all normal feelings so they don't have to feel that particular emotion they're trying to avoid. So the substitute feeling comes from "outside," most likely sex, drugs, or alcohol. Indulging recklessly or thoughtlessly in these three things is probably the most common way to avoid feeling any real emotion. Some people also use their work as substitute feeling, and we call them workaholics. And some even use excessive sports for distraction, like overly strenuous running or aerobics.

Whatever the substitute, it becomes addictive. Since it's the only way the person can get any "feeling" of being alive, he or she must turn to it over and over. But what a price to pay for avoiding pain! Not only is this person losing contact with their own soul - with real, true, authentic feelings of joy which could be theirs - not only is this person denied any real pleasure beyond the fleeting moments of empty gratification, but this person is getting set up for physical disease. That buried *real* feeling they're going to so much trouble to avoid is sitting inside them like a time bomb. It will "go off" one day and can take form in their body.

This pattern of addiction is so unnecessary when we realize that painful energy is our true, original ki energy in disguise. We don't want to cut it off! Everything we experience is connected to the original life force we all share. Everything we experience can be returned to our original ki, transformed into the original brightness and bliss that is the nature of our Silent Master Consciousness.

You have a right to health and wholeness! Right this moment, you are vibrating with the life force of the universe, the original ki that transformed into everything you presently see and experience. Don't be afraid to dance with your Silent Master energy! Embrace it confidently, looking forward to its power to transform every negative coloration in your life back into its original purity!

Exercises

1. *Dissolve a Negative Energy Pattern*. In this chapter we have looked at four steps to identify and ultimately dissolve an undesirable energy pattern. Why not try taking these four steps yourself to eliminate some life problem rooted in an energy distortion?

    i. Accept the emotion or belief (once you have identified it), and don't try to deny it or cut it off. Remember, it's your own energy that's been distorted.

    ii. Explore it by looking for other information contained in it. When you entertain this emotion or belief, what other feelings and ideas does it trigger? What behaviors do you enact because of it? What effects do those behaviors create in your experience, short term and long term?

    iii. Discharge the undesirable energy pattern by allowing yourself to feel it with full force, perhaps writing about it, talking about it, listening and looking to all areas of your life it impacts.

    iv. Take positive action to replace the negative energy pattern with a more desirable one, and put this new pattern into motion.

2. *Become Your Own Energy Doctor*. Do you have a physical health problem? Articulate what your particular problem is, and pay close attention to the words you use to describe your symptoms. These words may lead you to the roots of the problem in one of your other bodies. If you pay attention to the energy state of your symptoms, you can take appropriate action to bring your bodies into balance.

For instance, if you say something like: "I have this chronic rash that pops up now and again to make me miserable. It itches and makes me feel really angry and irritable. When it's acting up, I don't want to be around other people, and I have to drag myself to work."

There are several clues in this language that the problem originates in the emotional, mental, and spiritual bodies. The spiritual body is feeling an energy "drain"(*dragging* to work) most likely related to job dissatisfaction, and the physical body is manifesting the picture of this mental and emotional discord with a rash. Although it seems the rash makes the person angry and irritable, more likely the anger is originally due to some unresolved personality difficulties in the workplace, which is also creating the desire to leave the job. Something has gotten "under his or her skin," and the itching and scratching is the physical picture of the person's desire to get rid of the difficulty. Looking at the rash in this light, the person can take appropriate action to dissolve the problem at its roots.

Watch your language for help in healing energy problems. What is it you "can't stomach" or that's "hard to swallow"? What's the real "pain in the neck"? What's the major "headache" in your life? What's "eating you up"? What can't you "eliminate"? Where can't you be "flexible"? Where are you "unbending"? Where are the "knots" in your life, the "stumbling blocks," the "disintegration's"?

Meditation

My Silent Master awareness
is my pure, original, undistorted energy.
I allow this energy to transform
into my emotions,
shining with peace, joy,
bliss, and tranquillity...
into my thoughts and ideas
expressing love, generosity,
abundance, and completeness...
into my physical body
reflecting health, wholeness,
unity, and balance...
When I move,
I express the grace, beauty, agility,
flexibility, strength, and power
of my spiritual body.
When I rest,
I feel the free and open space
of my Silent Master awareness.
I perceive energy distortions
in myself and others with detachment.
I recognize the constantly changing nature of
feelings, thoughts, and circumstances,
and I allow my true energy
to transform all distortions
back into their original pure energy.

CHAPTER SIX

Ki and Taking Charge

You are who I dreamed of...
And so you came to be.
And you shall be with me beyond time.
I will never leave you,
and
My love will follow you
As you follow my Light,
Just as the tail of the bird follows the wing.

Be an Actor and a Creator

The ultimate goal of learning about your energy is so you can take charge of it! And the goal of taking charge of your energy is to live your life as an actor and creator, not a re-actor and a victim. Recently I had the pleasure of knowing someone who turned a possible victim scenario into a creative victory - all by taking charge in a situation rather than giving up. He proved that your own energy is yours to *direct*. Knowing this can make a big difference between victory and defeat.

Before the National Windsurfing Championships a number of years ago, a coach brought his entire windsurfing team to my school for a week of training. My purpose was to rev up their "winning" energy on all levels: body, mind, emotion, and spirit.

Phil was one of the team, an accomplished windsurfer, but quite a wild young man. Perhaps he had learned to ride the wind so well because that's the way he lived his life, moving from beach to beach, rarely staying in one place more than a week. He had no career other than windsurfing, no other training or education, and had finished only one book in his life. That was my first book, <u>Seven Steps to Inner Power</u>, which the coach required the team to read.

When Phil came to my school the first day, it was obvious he had no interest in all this "energy stuff," and he was complying with the coach only to stay on the team. But what a surprise he got when he started responding to some of my energy exercises, feeling a heightened state of alertness, expanding his awareness without losing focus, and experiencing relaxation without losing speed! Enjoying this new perception of his own energy, he was awakening to see that he could feel and integrate more of himself into his mind and body. And this was giving him a feeling of centered, calm control which would undoubtedly be reflected in his sport.

Plus, Phil was stimulated by the questions I put to the team to broaden their concept of themselves and their place in the universe. He had never thought it important to pursue questions about the nature of reality, but here he was doing it and finding that he had the ability to reach greater depths of understanding. This gave him even more confidence in himself.

Finally, the week of training was over, and the day of the national competition arrived. In the competition, each member of the team saw their week's work blossom into exceptional performance, many outperforming their personal best.

After Phil's first few heats, it looked like he, too, would see the fruit of his labors in outstanding performance. He was doing better than he'd ever done before and was now in the running to win. The week long energy training had given him an awareness of a calm, detached place within that flows like a quiet river...It's that somewhat meditative state which every athlete loves to feel and tries to maintain...where every movement flows at the right time, in the right way, with the right force.

This was the last heat, and all the racers were circling the mark waiting for the start. But just a short moment after the start, the current champion careened into Phil's board, capsizing him!

Everything tempted Phil at moment to sink into "Why me?!" anger and resentment. After all, he was so close to winning, and now this...this totally unfair situation seemed to be the cause of losing what he'd worked so hard to gain. It seemed everything was shouting, "It's over...may as well give up now..."

But instead, as he later told me, he heard my last words playing in his mind: *Nothing will stand in your way, not the weather, not the conditions, not the other sailors, not equipment problems, nothing...no matter what, you will rise above it, you will take charge!*

He got up, righted the board, and took off! He focused only on his goal and transformed his emotional state into that calm, detached state of mind.

The pack was way ahead of him by now. But setting his sights far beyond the leaders, ever so slowly he passed those in the rear, each inch moving him forward to his goal, each gain premeditated and determined. One by one he passed the other sailors, willing the board faster, pushing the sail with his own desire and drive. No anger, no fear, no frustration. Just focus and concentration.

In the last stretch of the race he pulled into the center of the leaders...then in the very last seconds, inched out into the lead to take the National Windsurfing Championship! In that moment Phil truly felt what it is to take charge of your life, to be master of the moment, master of his body, mind and emotions. Buddha said to his disciples one day in a bamboo grove:

> The one who has conquered himself is
> a far greater hero than the one who
> has defeated a thousand times a
> thousand men.

Imagine Phil's enjoyment of this victory! To win, he had to first conquer himself and prove he could master his body, mind, spirit, and emotions under stress, directing them with calmness and precision towards his goal. When he proved this to himself during the competition, he could now apply his skill to *any* important goal.

Conquering yourself, which means you're no longer a victim of your own negative energy, you are *free*! Then, with your freedom, you can share your strength creatively with everyone, helping them on their way to freedom just by being who you are. As Buddha says, this is the true, most powerful way of being a hero. Not by defeating others, but by strengthening yourself and others with your own constructive energy.

Too much of the time we feel controlled by forces outside us, when in fact, the goal of life is to realize that all those "forces" are made of the same energy we are. We are one with this energy and we can participate with it; we can transform and direct it instead of letting it just act on us. What is it you want to do: act or react?

In this chapter we're going to look at some attitudes and principles which promote the healthy, constructive use of your energy so that you are the one taking charge of your energy - not something or someone else. Are you ready to take charge of your life? Let's do it now!

Be the Owner of Your Life

I have an expression which I share with my students: *Be the owner of your life...don't rent yourself out!* One of the strongest marks of becoming an adult is becoming the driver in your life. When you're a child, it's appropriate to ask those who take care of you, *What do you want me to do? Where do you want me to go? How do you want me to behave?* But when you become an adult, it is appropriate to make the transition into deciding these things for yourself.

Unfortunately, many of us still live a left-over lifestyle made up of things determined and passed on by other people. When we become adults, we go on still trying to meet the expectations of everyone else, often sacrificing our true desires in the process. Of course, to some extent you must still meet the expectations of employers, teachers, or anyone invested with the responsibility of guiding you. But asking your employer *What do you want me to do?* is a far different issue than asking your wife, child, mother, friends, or acquaintances. With your employer it may be appropriate, but in the other instances, it may be dependency and avoiding responsibility.

It may also be painful. Dan, one of my students, was working in a family owned construction business which his parents expected him to do. He had even sort of managed to convince himself he "wanted" to do it, although now he was experiencing a chronic fatigue problem. He was wondering if he had one of those viral diseases that continually sap your energy and will until you feel quite weak and apathetic.

But as it turned out, as he got more in touch with his real feelings through energy training, with or without a virus, he realized he was very *unhappy* doing work for which he had no inspiration or desire! The closer he felt to his Silent Master Consciousness, the more uncomfortable he was being in this place. Finally, to save himself, he had to confront his father and leave the business to seek new career training in graphic arts, his true love. Dan felt such an energy boost in making this decision that he forgot all about any "virus." The fatigue disappeared almost immediately.

Until Dan made this decision, he was not being true to his own values. He was renting himself out. When he reclaimed the *ownership* of his life, he treated his physical, emotional, mental, and spiritual bodies to a surge of energy he hadn't felt in a long time. Why? He was letting in the ki energy of his Silent Master, his true, original self. The result was healing - physically, emotionally, mentally, and energetically. It is appropriate to do this, as I mentioned, and one of the characteristics of being an adult rather than a child is the courage to be your original self.

Doesn't a flower bloom just by being true to its own nature? What if it tried to be a potato for some reason? Wouldn't this be a senseless waste of energy? It takes far less effort to be your original self and far more energy to fight against your true reality.

In truth, you can't *really* fight it. You can only go through a lot of wasteful motion, whipping up a lot of effort and self-deception, only to end up losing anyway. Your Silent Master is always pressing to emerge, sometimes gently, sometimes forcefully, but *always in some way* to keep you moving toward an awareness of your real self. Why experience the pain of avoiding your real self if you don't have to? Instead, actively search for the real part of you, your Silent Master, so that you can relax into your true being. Maybe this is happening to you right now. This moment, listen to how you feel...how you really feel.

Since You're the Owner, Be the Driver

We are bombarded by so much aggressive influence from outside sources - billboards, televisions, blaring radios, pushy people, on and on - that it takes effort to remain true to yourself. Your best intentions won't do. Work does. You must exert effort.

Think about the process of buying a car. Since it's a large purchase, you most likely invest considerable planning into the process. You research, you talk to qualified sellers and owners, you shop around, you look in more than one place or more than one source, you examine your financial condition and all the areas this purchase will impact. Then, because your car is something personal and special, you put a lot of thought into the aesthetic values: the color, style, make, size, year...Think about all this energy you're exerting just to buy a car.

Aren't you just as valuable? Doesn't your life deserve equal energy for planning, research, and development? But ask yourself seriously how much attention you give yourself to think about goals, plans, secret desires, and how much time you spend actually putting forth a plan to reach your goals. Don't be surprised if the time spent purchasing a car wins!

There's not much in our education, formal or informal, which encourages us to think about ourselves this way. Instead, most of our education trains us how to fit into molds which already exist rather than creating new ones. We are born with our own mold, our Silent Master. That is the only one we need to worry about filling. But again, regaining an awareness, feeling and experience of our real self, usually requires effort. Let's recall Silent Master Image Five in my book, _Seven Steps to Inner Power_:

V

YOU HAVE THE POWER TO FULFILL YOUR DREAMS
_Your Silent Master is completely
aware, infinitely Intelligent, and_

> *ready to give you all the insight,*
> *information, and direction you need*
> *to fulfill your dreams, ambitions, and*
> *goals. In fact, this Consciousness is*
> *the Source of all your true desires.*

If you have the feeling of "drifting" through life right now, with no clear sense of your real purpose or direction, you simply have not heard the voice of your Silent Master. When you touch this part of yourself with awareness, which is the goal of working with your energy and purifying it, you begin to feel new desires, new intentions, new needs, and you feel impelled to take new actions. You won't always understand why you're feeling some of these new sensations, but they have their purpose, which ultimately does become visible to you. Your life purpose becomes visible, and all kinds of changes begin to manifest, leading you to fulfill that purpose.

At this point, when you're ready to become the driver of your life, you need to employ your energy in planning, organizing, and executing your goals. Before you may have been an on-again off-again driver with no clear direction. With your Silent Master Consciousness, you have both: the ability to drive, and a clear direction to take.

Making Choices Is a Powerful Use of Energy

Being a driver or actor means you will definitely have to make choices on your road to fulfillment. Instead of just drifting along like a piece of wood on a river, you actually direct your life by choosing this event, that path, this person, that area, on and on. This may sound overly simplistic, and you may be thinking, *"You don't have to tell me to make choices...I do it all the time."*

Next time you're feeling anxious, question whether or not you're holding back on some action you need to take or desire to take because you're afraid to choose. Fear comes in all kinds of forms and is usually paralyzing in some way. Often fear convinces us that it's easier to take a stance where we let things happen *to us*, when instead we could take a directed action leading to a preferred outcome.

One of the reasons we hold back on making choices is because we delude ourselves into thinking we already have chosen something. Let's say you don't have the employment you desire. You don't like where you are, but you're afraid to make a move. So you struggle along making yourself accept the situation, telling yourself you could leave if you *chose* to, all the while knowing you have no intentions of leaving. You simply go on feeling uncomfortable, unhappy, and anxious.

This is a classic example common to many of us where we say we have made a choice. But actually, it's pretty plain that the *real choice* remains unmade, frozen in fear. Beware of deluding yourself. Beware of convincing yourself you've *made* a choice, when in actuality you've only *accepted* a course of action.

Also, sometimes we tend to feel that making choices limits our options, and that by choosing a direction, we somehow eliminate all others. No. Quite the contrary, every time you make a choice, you *open up* an entire web of possibilities connected with that choice. If you dislike the outcome, the worst thing that happens is you make another choice, and this opens up another entire web of possibilities adding to all the possibilities of your previous choice! There is no limitation in choosing.

Follow Through with Goal Setting

After you've made a choice, give it a chance to come true! Give yourself a chance to realize your desire by setting specific goals and charting a specific course. Daydreaming and wishing are not goal setting. A goal is something that can be realized when you follow through with appropriate action. Here are some principles I use in setting goals that I want to fulfill.

First, and most important, make your goals *realistic*. Here you will have to use your own judgment and follow the inner direction of your Silent Master. Only you know what's truly within the parameters of your life purpose. As I just mentioned in Silent Master Image Five, all of us are born with a specific purpose to fulfill, and we already possess the potential to fulfill it. That's why we can follow our true desires, which will attract to us all the tools we need to do our work.

One criterion you can use in determining whether or not your goal is realistic is this: Is the desire that is driving you *your own*? Or is it based on the expectations of someone else? If you can honestly say that your desire is your own (not something you conjured up to please someone else), then even if it seems presently out of reach, you owe it to yourself to pursue it! Your Silent Master does not give you true desires for nothing. In fact, that is one way your Silent Master communicates with you and attempts to give you direction.

Then, once you have your goal, make it measurable somehow so that you know when you've reached it. Again, that may sound overly simplistic, but you may be amazed at how you refrain from doing this on a regular basis. We tend to state our goals vaguely and loosely like: *Yes, I'm going to lose weight*...or, *My new goal is to find a different job*...or, *I'm going to move soon*...How much weight are you going to lose and by when? What kind of job do you want, in what area, in what salary range, and by what date? Where are you going to move, to what kind of dwelling, for what price range, and by what date? If some of these parameters are open-ended, fine...but at least include them in your goal.

Set up milestones along the path to realizing your goal, ways you can check your progress. There are usually *steps* that you will take to fulfill a goal, and as you reach each step you can determine if you're truly moving forward or if you like where you're going. For instance, if your goal is to find a new job, one of your milestones may be simply getting a resume printed. Another might be finding an agency to help you.

Another might be getting some interviews in an area you like. At each of these points, you will be able to evaluate your progress and make changes if necessary.

Choosing milestones, of course, is part of forming your plan. You can't overlook the fact that you must proceed in some kind of orderly fashion, and this nearly always means forming a *planned* procedure to take. Here you will see the power of choice at work. One choice about what action to take opens up a whole range of other choices. Your first choice will lead you to the next step and the next if you just make a start!

You may want to actually make a contract with yourself to really sew up your plans! I often recommend to students that they write out an "agreement" which states the goal specifically, outlines steps they will take, sets milestones they will encounter, and the terms of fulfillment. Then I ask them to sign it and read it as often as possible. The content of the agreement must permeate all four bodies: physically in the actions you take, mentally in your thoughts, emotionally in your feelings, and spiritually in your dreams, aspirations and subconscious mind.

Try to be aware at the beginning of your path of what might arise to hinder you along the way. This is not asking for trouble, looking for trouble, or expecting trouble. It is, in fact, a way of helping avoid trouble. When you become aware of possible obstacles, you give some thought in advance as to how you will deal with them.

And what happens when you don't reach your goal the way you stated it or planned it? Keep going. Being half way there is better than where you were before you set the goal. Give yourself credit and praise for the effort you've made, and keep going. It doesn't matter how far behind you think you are in the race. And this leads me to another principle that's very important in taking charge of your life: avoid excuses.

Are you starting to feel like taking some constructive action? I hope the answer is a loud, resounding "yes!" Action is a necessary part of every goal you set and intend to fulfill.

Excuses Are a Senseless Waste of Energy

When a goal is taking longer than expected to fulfill, there is a strong temptation to give up and make excuses for failure. Your excuses prevent you from doing the additional work you need to do for ultimate success. Have you had the experience of saying *I know I should or shouldn't...whatever...but I'm doing it because...* I hear things from my students like *I know I shouldn't keep spending my money on gambling bets...but, (then the excuse)...*or, *I know I should tell my wife I've been seeing someone else...but, (then the excuse)...*or, *I know I should be exercising more...but, (then the excuse)...*

In all these instances, you do know the right thing to do, but you make an excuse! You make the excuse because somehow you think this is more beneficial than being honest with yourself or someone else. The next time you find yourself doing this, take one more step. Actually list the pros and cons of continuing lying to yourself alongside the pros and cons of being honest. I think you'll see on the "honest" side, you open up the possibility to actually *solve* a problem, even though there might be some conflict; and on the "dishonest" side you set yourself up to *continue* the problem at the price of avoiding conflict.

Most excuses are fueled by the belief that you *can't* do what you know you should. No such thing! Be aware that *I can't* usually means *I could, but I won't*. *I can't stop spending my money on gambling bets* usually means *I could stop, but I won't because I want the rush I get when I do it*. Or, *I can't work any harder to get this promotion* might mean *I could work harder, but I won't because I'm too lazy*.

In both these instances, we can see that the persons saying *I can't* have a problem with their self concept, not with their capability. In the gambler's situation, his or her addiction to the "rush" is most likely taking the place of genuine emotion that's buried (as we discussed in Chapter Five). He or she needs to rediscover the natural energy of real feeling, not the insubstantial "rushes" of gambling. Lazy persons most likely have some fear regarding their ability to achieve. They use laziness to avoid testing themselves and confronting their fear of failure.

So my point is, if you find yourself saying *I can't*, examine this statement very closely! It rarely means *I'm not able*, and your Silent Master is prepared to boost you and support you towards realizing any true desire you have. Most of the time, *you can!* You will just have to persevere with continued effort.

Energy in Motion Is Energy in Process

Some people never take their goals beyond "information collecting." They talk about what they want, they think about it, they look into it, they dream about it, they read books about it, they admire it...but they don't do anything about it! Remember, we live in a universe that's made of vibrating energy. Energy is in motion! We're part of that energy, and we need to express motion in our creativity. Fulfilling your goals requires an energy *process* to manifest - motion and activity! And the process is one that will most likely take place over time.

Unfortunately, we are bombarded by the media with images and slogans of instant gratification. "You want this...just call so and so *now*..." Or, "You want to look like this, be like this...just buy such and such *now*." Something I often tell my students is: *What you get easily, you can usually lose easily.* Even though as a rule we don't take advertising seriously, we are still impacted by these images to some extent. We are easily disappointed with delay when we pursue our goals, often using it as an excuse to give up.

Patience in today's world is not something that comes easily and naturally, and is something we generally need to *acquire*. That's partly because modern technology has given us a measure of instant gratification. Today when we want food, for instance, we can have it instantly at the supermarket, at a fast food drive-in, or at a restaurant. But there was a time when we had to patiently watch over our crops as they grew, milk the cows, pump the water, make the preserves, bake the bread, and so on. There was no room for impatience in that life.

You can take advantage of all of today's instantaneous resources - such as information technology and communications - to help you along the path toward your goal. But there is no substitute for old-fashioned patience in your pursuits. Not everything will be simply handed to you in a spoon-fed manner. There will almost always be a process involved in realizing your goals, a series of many steps that seemingly start and stop.

Keep in mind that the plateaus you reach on the way are not stopping points. They are just plateaus. It's important to remember that you are still in motion while you are seemingly "at rest." This can be very difficult to comprehend. It's like the people strapped into their airplane seats saying "I want to go somewhere, I want to go somewhere!" It may be hard to convince them that they are going somewhere.

When you are seemingly not in motion, it's important to keep your mind moving. Remember, when the seed is underground, invisible, it is nevertheless moving rather aggressively. And although you don't see the motion of the plant growing above the soil, it is nevertheless occurring.

In the same way, not all of your path will involve radical physical activity. Sometimes your faith and desire will be all you see in motion. But it is motion, it is going somewhere, and you will need patience to ride through to the end. To some extent, the total picture will always be a little outside your scope of vision. You'll have to trust in the power of your Silent Master to guide you to and through the unseen steps involved.

As for a delay in reaching your goal, remember it's not over 'til it's over. As long as you're here, the opportunity to reach your goal is here! Keep on going!

Letting Go Invites New Energy Into the Picture

Never forget that when you reach for the new - in the form of a new goal you're trying to realize - it may be necessary to let go of the old, the past, the outmoded. You may have to think about changing your look, your environment, some of your friends and acquaintances, and unhealthy values, attitudes, and motivations. Are you willing to do that?

If you hear yourself saying, "Yes, yes, I'm willing!" then test yourself by doing it. Find out how easily you can give up elements in your life that are detrimental to your present goal. That will tell you something about the strength of your commitment.

In Chapter Three I described one of my students who had to completely change the detrimental aspects of her environment to change her life. Remember, she was somewhat surprised at how difficult it was to give up these familiar things, even though she knew they would probably interfere with her goal. In the same way, you may find yourself strongly tempted to not rock the boat when you feel that initial discomfort in creating change.

I always remember the caterpillar when thinking about this subject of letting go. It's such a beautiful example of transformation! Just as you do, the caterpillar has a process to go through in fulfilling his goal, one seemingly fraught with obstacles, risks, and delay. Yet, there is no giving up as he follows his inner instincts - just like the inner instincts your Silent Master gives you - as day by day he goes about his routine crawling from leaf to leaf. Since he is completely in tune with his own life force, he knows when it's time to stop.

Very importantly, when this time of his *change* comes about, he does not attempt to cling to the old form simply because it is familiar. He lets go of the old, again trusting and following his instincts, and willingly endures a plateau of seeming inaction while a wondrous, creative transformation slowly manifests! Is the caterpillar patient? Isn't he simply being true to himself? Isn't patience simply being true to yourself? Isn't transformation simply being true to yourself? Isn't letting go simply being true to yourself?

I think the answer is yes to all. When you are true to yourself, you let in the energy that transforms you and everything around you, fulfilling the goal you set, planned, followed, and have now realized!

You Are One with All the Power in the Universe

Wake up to the little miracles around you right now and appreciate the power of the universal life force! This is your power we're talking about, and your intelligence.

Look again at our caterpillar. Imagine trying to explain this miraculous transformation to someone who had never heard of it. You talk about a worm-like crawling bug who eats plants, but who knows when he's eaten enough and when it's time to stop, who knows how to wrap himself with threads that he makes from his own body, who then disappears inside this sealed encasement, who then secretes chemicals from his own body which let him disassemble and re-form again - not as a drab crawling bug, but as a multicolored winged creature that flies through the air! This doesn't sound like it should be possible, does it? Such creativity...such intelligence...such *imagination*!

Or, how about the giant stars out there, exploding into elements that "know how" to form as the metals and minerals of planets...The incredible, unspeakable power of a black hole that holds an entire galaxy in orbit...Or, think about the cells from a man and woman that unite and know how to express themselves as eyes, hands, hair, legs, feet, ears, and a brain that processes intangible qualities like feelings, thoughts, desires, and love...Or the tiny little brown nut that holds within it the awesome power to transform into a majestic tree! If all this does not begin to convince you how creative the universal life force is, think again.

This very creativity is your own! These miracles we take for granted every day are pictures of your own life force in motion. How can you still insist that you are nothing, nobody, with no purpose, no talent, when you possess energy like this? A tiny unborn bird pecks away at his shell hundreds of times for no other reason than to be born! For no other reason than to be who he is. He follows the life force as far as his purpose directs.

But you! You are born with so much more capability than this little bird. If you are not living your life with the same enthusiasm of a supernova, exploding to fill your space with energy to build and create and transform, you are still inside a dark shell. If you are sitting around doing nothing more than feeling sorry for yourself, then you're not even as true and honest as the little bird, who at least honors his life force by pecking his way out into the world.

Ki Is the Key to Freedom!

I'm asking you to come out and start appreciating this life force that brought you here! I'm asking you to start honoring the power which is your birthright, and the responsibility you have to fulfill yourself with this energy. Yes, it is a responsibility, because when you refuse to be yourself, you cheat the universe out of a part of itself. You are here now because you have a purpose that is part of the entire universal expression. To do your part, all you have to do is to just *be yourself*, your true self, and honor yourself with love, support, training, perseverance, and fulfillment!

I'm asking you to do something that is actually easier than being untrue to yourself! Think how much pain and effort it takes to make yourself live out of sync with your true desires...keeping a relationship that's wrong...doing unchallenging work...making money that goes nowhere, accomplishing nothing. Living wrongly takes enormous energy! When all of your energy goes to non-constructive purposes, you feel drained and apathetic. That's why you say you're "*sick and tired*" of living this way.

You can make a change! One of the main points I've tried to make throughout this book is that your ki energy is transforming energy. That is its very nature. It transforms and manifests in different ways, shapes and forms according to your direction. The picture of your body and environment right now is a result of how you have directed your energy up to now. The picture you see right now didn't exist until it transformed into this picture. And if you choose, it can transform again!

You are not stuck in one "place." You are never stuck, because everything around you is in motion, vibrating in constant change. Have the courage to change your mind and emotions. Have the courage to examine yourself, the beliefs you hold, the emotions you feel, and be willing to purify your energy. Have the courage to try! Then you will see change all around you.

How fortunate we all are to be learning about the energetic nature of our world. This is the key to our freedom because we realize everything that exists as energy can be shaped! We never have to be a victim of what we see, because what we see is energy that can be changed. Our oneness with the entire energetic fabric of the universe means we are participating in everything that manifests. We are co-creators of the world we live in, and what we think, feel, say, and do *matters*!

We like to say how much we value freedom. If that is true, then we must *be* free and *act* free by directing our energy with love, enthusiasm, and responsibility! Knowing, as we do, that energy is the essence of the universe, we are in a position to be builders and creators, not merely followers of old, outmoded values. It's time to give up apathy and lethargy, come out of our dark shell of fear, and let our freedom inspire our brothers and sisters to desire the same.

Your Silent Master Is Smiling

There was the Bronze Age, the Iron Age...I call this the Stress Age. Not that life is stressful only in this century. All epochs have had their own unique stresses, but the difference now is that danger, stress, and warfare were more localized in previous times. Today we have weaponry that can bring about *total global destruction*. Although we don't consciously think about this on a daily basis, for the most part, this potential threat hangs in our atmosphere, misting down into our collective mind feelings of anxiety, cynicism, dread, fear. Relaxation, simple joy, peaceful contentment are not typical qualities of our global citizens. Economic stress, famine, civil wars, mass murder...our planet is filled with much sorrow and distress.

Yes, we need to be concerned about any and all issues that arise concerning our capability to live together without mutual destruction. Yes, we need to take intelligent personal, social, or political action where appropriate or where we are guided to do so. But all the stresses of the modern world are not reasons to live in fear!

Remember, our main responsibility is to discover and express who we really are. When we find our Silent Master within, and express our pure, original joy, peace, harmony and truth, we are a stabilizing energy presence wherever we are. Energy impacts energy as we discussed in Chapter Three. Our energy impacts the energy "out there." The energy of our natural strength and joy is unaffected by the changing picture outside us, and instead, we are the instruments that change the picture! In order to allow our energy to change the picture we see, we remain detached.

As I mentioned previously, detachment is not a cold, lifeless, dry state of mind. It is a vibrant state of radiating love! Detachment means you act rather than react, and your action is that of radiating the pure qualities of your Silent Master.

When we see images of Buddha, for instance, smiling detachedly in meditation while the world outside is possibly in turmoil, this doesn't mean that Buddha is ignorant of suffering or has no compassion. It means he knows that the essence of his Silent Master Consciousness - in its pure, undistorted form - is *love*, smiling, peaceful love. He knows that if he wants to help the world in turmoil, heal the world, and change the world, the power of his high energy love radiated into the world is the most powerful, far-reaching influence he can exert. Energy impacts energy! Love is the highest and most powerful energy that exists. It can transform the entire world. Would you like to participate in this transformation? You can! You are needed!

Gratitude Is Love in Action

But first you can transform yourself with love! A very powerful expression of love is simple gratitude. Why is gratitude powerful? When you express gratitude, you are acknowledging that something good exists. This action energizes that good thing and gives it momentum to continue existing. One way to love yourself and bring about the changes you desire is to use the power of gratitude.

By making gratitude a part of your conscious everyday life, you are energizing the good you want to attract. What do you have that you want to keep? Whatever it is, consciously express gratitude for it. This keeps it alive and vibrating in your experience.

Gratitude can be one of the best transformational tools you have, and may be one of the easiest to use. What do you not have that you want to attract? What do you want to transform? Since you don't presently have this thing, consciously express gratitude for the *idea* of whatever you want. The idea itself, as we discussed previously, already has some energy that wants to manifest. When you express gratitude for this idea, you lend even more energy to it, and it has even more momentum to materialize.

Gratitude is a certain *poise* more than an action, an *attitude* more than a string of words. Gratitude takes many forms. You express gratitude when you appreciate, when you praise, when you give generously, when you love, when you are affectionate, when you admire, when you clean, when you accept others' gifts to you thankfully, when you help, when you cooperate, when you laugh, when you are jubilant, when you are happy, when you express something from your heart, even when you create something beautiful, and most importantly, when you are just true to yourself, completely honest in being your real self!

These are just some of the ways to start using gratitude. There are even more ways to be grateful for the infinite potential you have! One way is to experience great loss in some form. I was five years old during the Korean War and had the misfortune of seeing my small friend killed right in front of me. Although I had other sorrows and misfortunes in my childhood, this event always helped me remember to be grateful for what I *did* have, no matter how small. Often we see celebrities who seem to "have it all," but who also experience loss or tragedy of some kind. Nobody is above sorrow in life, and we need to remain grateful for every bit of good we have or would like to have!

Seek Your Infinite Potential Fearlessly

The nature of material life is that pleasure and pain, happiness and sadness, coexist and constantly change from one to the other. That is the nature of this world. No matter which polarity you are feeling at this moment, your Silent Master Consciousness is still shining with purity, love, wholeness, peace, and joy.

We might be tempted to think that in times of happiness, perhaps it's easier to discover our Silent Master

Consciousness. Not necessarily. Sometimes material happiness keeps us very attached to material possessions, and it's not until we experience pain or loss that we seek a different, more enduring point of view.

Your Silent Master Consciousness does not fluctuate between happiness and sadness, gain and loss, joy and sorrow. It is the eternal, unchanging bliss of your pure being, your original self! It never "goes away." But you can go away from it by refusing to be aware of it.

Your Silent Master Consciousness gives you awareness of everything you need to remain fearless, and gives you the power to change any and all circumstances confronting you!

How much energy are you spending on being afraid right now? How much energy are you using to avoid confronting your fears, darting from one unsuccessful circumstance to another? How much energy are you using settling for "quick fixes" that have never worked out? Aren't you ready to just be who you are, feel your power to fulfill yourself, and live out your true life purpose *freely* and *fearlessly*?

Then why not put the same amount of energy into discovering your Silent Master Consciousness, your true energy, the ki of the universal life force which breathes through you right now! You do not have to go anywhere to do this. The energy that you're expressing right now - no matter how much you do or don't like it - is your Silent Master energy colored by many beliefs, ideas, concepts, and emotions.

You can go through the process of purifying, brightening, and heightening your energy until you feel consciously at one with your Silent Master, with all that is, and feel yourself flow into the pattern that fulfills your highest potential, serving yourself, serving others, drawing your life force to its complete and beautiful expression here and now!

Go out and look at the sun. Really be aware of that incredible brightness, the energy that is radiating from ninety-three million miles away. The same energy that made that sun, made you. Think about that! You're not just a lump of clay, a collection of minerals and salts. You are connected to a power that is the creative life force of the universe, the same power that created that sun! Yet you are as beautiful and delicate as the rose, as fluid and powerful as white water rapids on a river, as transparent as the shifting colors of a sunset, as impenetrable as a mountain, as vast as the sky and its galaxies...You and all of this are made of the same energy. You are as natural as all these things and have the same right to exist complete and fulfilled as they do.

But there is one difference between you and these elements of nature. You have the gift of being able to direct this energy! You are not only the created, but a co-creator.

Are you ready to be who you are? Are you ready to start dancing with your energy, finally, at long last, creating the life you were meant to have? Think of it! You stand at the beginning of your life. Your story is just now being written! You can write your own adventure filled with all the drama, excitement, and passionate love you can imagine. We have completed Chapter One, entitled "I Find Out Who I Am." My love will go with you always.

Exercises

1. Now that you're ready to begin writing the next chapter of your life, this is a good time to get rid of any limitations that could hold you back from your true goals. Take a look now at your "I can't" statements and be willing to re-word them as "I could but I won't because..." Then provide your own solution with "I can if..." This exercise may show you how you're holding yourself back with your own beliefs - which *can* be replaced with better ones.

2. Here is a sample of a contract one of my students wrote in order to pursue his goals. Perhaps you can create one of your own.

I Can't...	I Could, but I Won't Because...	I Can If...
I can't swim.	I could swim, but I won't because I'm afraid of deep water.	I can swim if I choose to confront my fear and take swimming lessons.

Meditation

Every thought, idea, and feeling I have,
every element in my environment,
is flowing right now in constant change,
oscillating, vibrating, becoming new
at every instant in time.
This moment,
I am poised at the brink of a new creation,
a new world, a new thought, a new feeling,
a new idea, a new environment,
and a new relationship...
I seize this moment,
and right now I exercise my creative power to
manifest a new life.
Every element of my life forms and reforms
as I let go
and allow the perfect light
of my Silent Master awareness
to guide me into more harmonious perceptions,
deeper understandings,
and greater love.
I love my power to make every moment new...
I love my power to feel my unity
with my Silent Master awareness...
I love my power to guide the changes in my life so
they form
into peaceful, joyous manifestations.
I love myself and all persons unconditionally, and
am grateful for the ki energy
that gives life to everything
I create with my love.

The First Element

Index

Glossary

Air Energy

One of the four basic elements. Air energy is the breath of life. How we breathe influences us physically, emotionally, mentally, and spiritually. Also corresponds to our mental body, because air and ideas have the same infinitely expansive quality.

Chi

The Chinese word for Energy.

Earth Energy

One of the four basic elements. All material things in our world are made of earth energy.

Elements

The four basic elements are Earth, Water, Air, and Fire, corresponding to our Physical, Emotional, Mental, and Spiritual Bodies, respectively.

Emotional Body

The part of your energy field in which emotions occur. This body's element is Water. Like water, emotional energy should flow without obstruction.

Energy

This is the Life Force of the Universe, of which you are a part. It is the power that beats your heart and drives your every thought, feeling, and action. In its pure, undistorted form, it is Love.

Fire Energy

One of the four basic elements. Spiritual energy is fire energy. It is pure life force energy. It gives warmth and movement to your Physical Body, warmth to your Emotional Body, and awareness, insight, intelligence, and will to your Mental Body.

Hwa Gi

A meditation in which Buddhist monks sit in the winter snow in wet sheets, focusing on their fire

157

energy so intensely that they dry the sheets. Also called Inner Fire meditation.

Inner Eyes   The part of you that observes your own thoughts, feelings, and actions and knows your inner truth.

Jung SuWon   The way of uniting body, mind, and spirit in total harmony. A formal martial art, but also a way of life.

Ki, Gi, or Qi   The Korean word for Energy.

Life Force   The original Energy of the Universe. See Energy.

Love   The most basic characteristic of pure Life Force Energy.

Meditation   Bringing body, mind, and spirit to a single focus.

Mental Body   The part of your energy field in which thoughts and ideas occur. This body's element is Air. Air and ideas have the same infinitely expansive quality.

Original Self   Who you are before and beyond the ways in which your family and culture conditioned you. See Silent Master Consciousness.

Physical Body   The part of your energy field that you can see and feel. This body's element is Earth. Earth energy is the least permanent of our energies.

Prana   The Indian word for Energy.

Silent Master Consciousness   The Life Force of the Universe as it Occurs in you personally. Your true, original self.

Spiritual Body   The part of your energy field that is pure Life Force Energy. This body's element is Fire. Fire's characteristics are warmth and light: the warmth of Love and the light of infinite awareness.

Tan Jun   The Energy center just below your navel. When you breathe properly, you breathe into and out of your Tan Jun.

Tao   The Source of all, the "parent" of everything that exists potentially and everything that exists actually.

Water Energy   One of the four basic elements. Water energy flows over, under, around, or through any obstacles. It is gentle yet powerful. Water energy comprises your Emotional Body. Like water, emotional energy should flow without obstruction.

Yang   The energy of an active state... outward radiation, thrusting, expanding, giving, the positive condition of light.

Yin   The energy of a passive state... inward absorption, yielding, contracting, receiving, the negative condition of dark.

About the Author

Grandmaster Tae Yun Kim is the author of several books, creator of numerous audio and video tapes, host of internationally broadcast " The Grandmaster Kim Show," and a world renowned key note speaker. She is the recipient of the Susan B. Anthony Award, Woman of Achievement Award, and the prestigious Cultural Living Treasure of South Korea Award.

Additionally, Grandmaster Kim owns one of the largest wellness centers in the U.S. and is the founder of the popular art of Jung Su Won(the practice of uniting mind, body, and spirit for total harmony.)

Grandmaster Kim has taught thousands how to attain optimum levels of energy and peace by discovering their true selves. Using the strength of her ability to teach others how to tap into this empowerment, Grandmaster Kim continues to share her ancient secrets and profound techniques with people nationwide.

Product Catalog

B101, $11.95 <u>Seven Steps to Inner Power</u> *Book-* Provides an accelerated sampling of Grandmaster Tae Yun Kim's philosophy and teachings on how to succeed in the modern day world. Her motto, "He can do, She can do, why not me!" embodies her belief that every person has an incredible power just waiting to be tapped!

B104, $19.95 <u>Seven Steps to Inner Power Workbook</u> - Improve your career, relationships and health. Learn how to take charge of your life by setting and achieving goals through the exercises and self-assessments in this purposeful workbook.

B102, $10.95 <u>The Silent Master</u> *Book-* By following the Silent Master within, you can overcome any obstacle and rise above limitation. Each chapter outlines a different aspect of self-discovery and offers a specific lesson designed to put the concepts into action.

B103, $14.95 <u>The First Element: The Secrets to Maximizing Your Energy</u> *Book-* Grandmaster Tae Yun Kim explains ki energy in terms of your environment, your relationships with others, your health, and your ability to create the life you've always wanted.

V201, $29.95 <u>Seven Steps to Inner Power: Shim Gong</u> *Video* - Grandmaster Kim demonstrates the Seven Steps to Inner Power in this inspiring and action-packed video. Includes interviews of students who have used these principles to achieve outstanding results on the training floor and in their lives.

V202, $29.95 <u>The Power of Forms: Hyung</u> *Video* - This 60 minute video includes the most common Korean hard forms and traditional weapon forms, as well as many soft forms rarely seen before.

V203, $29.95 <u>Reaching Beyond the Ordinary: Nae Gong</u> *Video* - Grandmaster Kim demonstrates five ways of thinking that will improve your physical performance. This is the groundwork for the Seven Steps to Inner Power, presented in a video full of practical philosophy and spectacular action.

V204, $39.95 <u>Ki Rhythm</u> *Video* - This video takes you through step by step energy forms that help to reduce stress, focus on your goals, overcome obstacles, and increase your energy.

A301, $12.95 <u>Be Free</u> *Audio* - Virtually everyone has something that prevents them from being their best. Whether it's lack of confidence, fear, stress, anger, jealousy, or another negative emotion, we must learn to let go and learn to Be Free.

A302, $12.95 <u>Rising Above</u> *Audio* - Listen to the sounds of nature as Grandmaster Kim takes you through an inspiring meditation exercise designed to relieve stress and develop motivation.

A303, $12.95 <u>Be An Original</u> *Audio* - Follow Grandmaster Kim as she leads you through the process of eliminating self-doubt and lack of confidence. Develop a greater feeling of self-worth. Yes you can do it!

A304, $12.95 <u>Ocean Magic</u> *Audio-* Grandmaster Kim uses the power of the ocean along with a centuries-old meditation technique to produce an extremely relaxing and revitalizing mental state you can experience time and time again.

A305, $12.95 <u>Grandmaster's Song</u> *Audio-* An instrumental music track inspired by Grandmaster Tae Yun Kim that is designed to release anxiety, relieve stress and enhance clear thinking.

A306, $12.95 <u>New Dimensions</u> *Audio-* A radio talk show broadcast worldwide on the New Dimensions radio show. A dynamic one hour seminar with Grandmaster Tae Yun Kim on the topic of rising above your environment and the Seven Steps to Inner Power.

A307, $49.95 <u>Ki Energy</u> *Set of 6 Audio Tapes* - This meditation series is a collection of beautiful music sung by Grandmaster Kim. Designed to recharge your energy while meditating, working at a desk, preparing a meal, driving a car, relaxing, or before you go to sleep. You may notice that certain melodies will help you focus and energize your day.

A310, $24.95 <u>Seven Steps to Inner Power</u> *Book on Tape* - You can read *<u>Seven Steps to Inner Power</u>* or listen to it! Grandmaster speaks "between the lines" to add some extra surprises.

A311, $12.95 <u>Whisper to Your Soul</u> *Audio-* Soothing and uplifting flute music played by Grandmaster Tae Yun Kim. Designed to relax the body, calm the mind, and free the spirit.

These products are available from:

Quantity discounts are available on bulk purchases. For more information contact NorthStar.

NOTE: These products are not intended as a treatment for any physical or psychological disease. The author assumes no medical or legal responsibility for having the contents of these products considered as a prescription for anyone.

NORTHSTAR

119 Minnis Circle, Milpitas, CA 95035
1-800-565-8713 Fax (408) 942-0925
www.gonorthstar.com

Order Form

Item#	Qty	Description	Unit Price	Total

Charge: Visa / MC / AMEX EXP: #: DATE:	Subtotal	
Signature: Name (print):	Applicable Tax (CA Residents)	
Address:	*S/H (US only)	
City / State / Zip	TOTAL	

* Shipping/handling: $5.00 for the first item or set, add $2.00 for each additional item or set. International orders: S/H costs handled on a per order basis.

Make check or money orders payable to:

NORTHSTAR

119 Minnis Circle, Milpitas, CA 95035
1-800-565-8713 Fax (408) 942-0925
www.gonorthstar.com